The Cambridge Introduction to
Samuel Johnson

Samuel Johnson is a towering figure of eighteenth-century literature, 'arguably the most distinguished man of letters in English history' (*Oxford Dictionary of National Biography*). As well as the celebrated author of *A Dictionary of the English Language*, Johnson was the leading literary critic of his time, and a writer who contributed to almost every genre from poetry to political pamphleteering. At the same time, an enduring legend developed around him, culminating in James Boswell's classic biography. This book offers a concise introduction to Johnson's many-sided work, as well as explaining its historical context. Presenting Johnson in his different guises – journalist, poet and storyteller, scholar, critic, political and social thinker, biographer and legend – it guides the reader through Johnson's writings, including detailed treatments of his major texts.

Robert DeMaria, Jr has devoted most of his professional life to the study of Samuel Johnson. He is the author of three monographs on Johnson and the co-editor of three volumes as well as the general editor of *The Yale Edition of the Works of Samuel Johnson*, 23 vols. (1958–2018).

Dan Hitchens is a writer, journalist, and senior editor of *First Things*.

The Cambridge Introduction to
Samuel Johnson

ROBERT DEMARIA, JR
Vassar College

DAN HITCHENS

CAMBRIDGE
UNIVERSITY PRESS

Shaftesbury Road, Cambridge CB2 8EA, United Kingdom

One Liberty Plaza, 20th Floor, New York, NY 10006, USA

477 Williamstown Road, Port Melbourne, VIC 3207, Australia

314–321, 3rd Floor, Plot 3, Splendor Forum, Jasola District Centre,
New Delhi – 110025, India

103 Penang Road, #05–06/07, Visioncrest Commercial, Singapore 238467

Cambridge University Press is part of Cambridge University Press & Assessment, a department of the University of Cambridge.

We share the University's mission to contribute to society through the pursuit of education, learning and research at the highest international levels of excellence.

www.cambridge.org
Information on this title: www.cambridge.org/9781009534567

DOI: 10.1017/9781009534550

© Robert DeMaria, Jr & Dan Hitchens 2025

This publication is in copyright. Subject to statutory exception and to the provisions of relevant collective licensing agreements, no reproduction of any part may take place without the written permission of Cambridge University Press & Assessment.

When citing this work, please include a reference to the DOI 10.1017/9781009534550

First published 2025

A catalogue record for this publication is available from the British Library.

Library of Congress Cataloging-in-Publication Data
Names: DeMaria, Robert, Jr., 1948– author. | Hitchens, Daniel, 1989– author.
Title: The Cambridge introduction to Samuel Johnson / Robert DeMaria, Jr., Dan Hitchens.
Description: Cambridge ; New York, NY : Cambridge University Press, 2025. | Series: The Cambridge companions to literature | Includes bibliographical references and index.
Identifiers: LCCN 2024043288 | ISBN 9781009534567 (hardback) | ISBN 9781009534536 (paperback) | ISBN 9781009534550 (ebook)
Subjects: LCSH: Johnson, Samuel, 1709–1784. | Johnson, Samuel, 1709–1784 – Criticism and interpretation. | Authors, English – 18th century – Biography. | Lexicographers – Great Britain – Biography. | Critics – Great Britain–Biography. | LCGFT: Biographies. | Literary criticism.
Classification: LCC PR3533 .D38 2025 | DDC 828/.609 [B]–dc23/eng/20240926
LC record available at https://lccn.loc.gov/2024043288

ISBN 978-1-009-53456-7 Hardback
ISBN 978-1-009-53453-6 Paperback

Cambridge University Press & Assessment has no responsibility for the persistence or accuracy of URLs for external or third-party internet websites referred to in this publication and does not guarantee that any content on such websites is, or will remain, accurate or appropriate.

To
Joanne DeMaria
and
Peter and Eve Hitchens

Contents

List of Figures	*page* viii
Acknowledgements	ix
Chronology	x
List of Abbreviations	xiv

Chapter 1 Life and Times — 1

Chapter 2 Journalist — 23

Chapter 3 Poet and Storyteller — 43

Chapter 4 Scholar — 61

Chapter 5 Critic — 78

Chapter 6 Social and Political Thinker — 97

Chapter 7 Biographer — 115

Chapter 8 Legend — 133

Notes	150
Further Reading	156
Index	160

Figures

3.1 Johnson in his late thirties, from the mezzotint by George Zobel. © National Portrait Gallery, London. *page* 42
6.1 *Walking up the High Street* by Thomas Rowlandson. Courtesy of the Lewis Walpole Library, Yale University. 96
7.1 Johnson in 1775 by Sir Joshua Reynolds. © Courtesy of the Huntington Art Museum, San Marino, California. 114
8.1 Johnson about 1783 by John Opie. Courtesy of Houghton Library, Harvard University (82M-20). 132
8.2 Johnson's death mask, after William Cumberland Cruikshank. © National Portrait Gallery, London. 135

Acknowledgements

We would like to thank the first arbiter of this project, Linda Bree, and its patient parent, Bethany Johnson, as well as the anonymous outside readers, the copy editor, designers, typesetters, and others who gave our work 'a local habitation and a name' in the form of the book now in your hands.

Robert DeMaria writes: I would like to thank Joanne DeMaria, my partner in life and love for fifty years.

Dan Hitchens writes: Johnson referred to 'that love of life which is necessary to the vigorous prosecution of any undertaking'. So thank you to Amy and Conal, without whom this book might never have been finished. It would never have got started without my doctoral supervisor Freya Johnston, an encourager and mentor to so many students, who very characteristically suggested this project in the first place. And thanks above all to my first and greatest teachers, my parents, to whom this book is dedicated.

Chronology

Dates are Old Style (O.S.) until 1752, unless otherwise noted. Years, however, are all in New Style (N.S., i.e. beginning on 1 January). See the timelines of Pat Rogers, *The Samuel Johnson Encyclopedia* (Westport, CT: Greenwood Press, 1996) and Jack Lynch (ed.), *Samuel Johnson in Context* (Cambridge University Press, 2011) for further details.

1709	(7 September O.S.; 18 September N.S.) Samuel Johnson born in Lichfield to Michael and Sarah Johnson. Richard Steele begins publication of the *Tatler* (12 April). Alexander Pope begins his publishing career.
1712	Johnson touched for the 'King's Evil' (scrofula) in London by Queen Anne.
1714	Death of Queen Anne; George, Elector of Hanover, becomes George I of Great Britain (1 August).
1717	Enters Lichfield Grammar School.
1720	'South-Sea Bubble', a massive stock collapse.
1721	Robert Walpole becomes de facto prime minister.
1725	Extended stay in the household of his cousin Cornelius Ford in Stourbridge.
1726	*Gulliver's Travels* published.
1727–8	Self-directed reading at home in Lichfield; George I dies; George II is king (11 June 1727).
1728	Enters Pembroke College, Oxford, where he remains for thirteen months.
1729	Returns to Lichfield; fails to secure a teaching post.
1731	Death of Johnson's father, Michael Johnson, leaving scant provision for his survivors.

1732	Works for a few months as an usher (teaching assistant) at Market Bosworth School.
1732–3	Writing for the *Birmingham Journal*.
1735	Marries Elizabeth Jervis Porter, a widow twenty years his senior with three children; publishes *A Voyage to Abyssinia*, a translation of a Jesuit missionary's account.
1736	Starts his school at Edial; writes some portion of *Irene*.
1737	Johnson and Garrick go to London (2 March); only brother Nathaniel dies.
1738	Publishes *London*; writes the life of Paulo Sarpi, part of his abandoned translation of Sarpi's *History of the Council of Trent*.
1739	*Marmor Norfolciense*; *A Compleat Vindication of the Licensers of the Stage*.
1740	Lives of Blake, Drake, and Barretier; 'Essay on Epitaphs'; epitaph on Claudy Philips; prologue to Garrick's *Lethe*.
1741–3	*Debates in the Senate of Magna Lilliputia*.
1742	Life of Sydenham; resignation of Walpole.
1743	Catalogue of the Harleian Library; 'The Young Author' published; Richard Savage dies in debtors' prison; Henry Pelham becomes prime minister.
1744	*The Life of Richard Savage*; death of Pope (30 May).
1745	*Miscellaneous Observations on Macbeth*; death of Walpole; death of Swift (19 October).
1746	Signs contract to write *A Dictionary of the English Language*.
1747	*Plan of a Dictionary of the English Language*; *Drury-Lane Prologue* (15 September).
1748	Contributions to Robert Dodsley's educational text, *The Preceptor*.
1749	*The Vanity of Human Wishes*; *Irene*; William Lauder's essay on Milton; moves into the house in Gough Square.
1750–2	*The Rambler* (20 March 1750–14 March 1752)
1750	Francis Barber brought to England by his enslaver Richard Bathurst.
1751	*Life of Cheynel*.

1752	Death of Elizabeth Porter Johnson (17 March); Johnson writes dedication for Charlotte Lennox, *The Female Quixote*; Anna Williams takes up residence in Johnson's house. *The Adventurer* begins (7 November).
1753	Francis Barber comes to Johnson's household.
1753–4	Writes for John Hawkesworth's *Adventurer*.
1754	Life of Edward Cave, the proprietor and founder of the *Gentleman's Magazine*.
1755	*A Dictionary of the English Languages*; awarded MA by Oxford University.
1756	Edits Sir Thomas Browne's *Christian Morals* with a life of Browne.
1756–7	Contributions to *The Literary Magazine*; the life of Frederick the Great; Johnson meets Reynolds; Seven Years' War begins.
1757	Review of Soame Jenyns; John Wilkes elected to Parliament.
1758–60	*The Idler* (15 April 1758–5 April 1760).
1758	Briefly under arrest for debt; relieved by Samuel Richardson.
1759	*Rasselas*; mother dies in Lichfield (23 January); moves from Gough Square; Battle of Quebec.
1760	'Bravery of English Common Soldiers'; moves to 1 Inner Temple Lane; death of George II; George III is king (25 October).
1761	Edits Roger Ascham's *English Works*, with a life of Ascham; death of Samuel Richardson.
1762	Awarded an annual pension of £300 by George III.
1763	Meets James Boswell (16 May); Peace of Paris ending Seven Years' War.
1764	Forms The Club with Joshua Reynolds.
1765	Meets Hester and Henry Thrale (9 January); *The Plays of William Shakespeare*; awarded LLD degree by Trinity College Dublin; moves to a house in Johnson's Court; Wilkesite riot in St George's Fields, Southwark.
1766	Assists Robert Chambers on the Second Vinerian Law Lectures.
1767	Private meeting with King George III.
1768	Royal Academy founded.

1769	Garrick organizes the Shakespeare Jubilee in Stratford; Reynolds delivers his first *Discourse* at the Royal Academy; Captain Cook arrives in Tahiti.
1770	*The False Alarm*; birth of William Wordsworth.
1771	*Thoughts on Falkland's Islands*.
1772	Lord Mansfield's decision in Somerset v Stewart, an important step in the abolition of slavery.
1773	Tours Scotland with Boswell; revised editions of the *Dictionary* and the *Plays of William Shakespeare*.
1774	*The Patriot*; tour of North Wales with Thrales; Donaldson v Becket establishes that copyright is not perpetual.
1775	*A Journey to the Western Islands of Scotland*; visits France with Thrales and Baretti; birth of Jane Austen. LLD from Oxford University; Battle of Lexington and Concord.
1776	Johnson moves to his final dwelling place, No. 8, Bolt Court; Declaration of Independence in America.
1777	*The Convict's Address* and other writings for William Dodd.
1779	Death of Garrick.
1780	Gordon Riots in London.
1779–81	*Prefaces, Biographical and Critical to the Works of the English Poets*.
1781	*The Lives of the Poets* published independently.
1783	Suffers stroke (17 June).
1784	Hester Thrale marries Gabriel Piozzi (23 July); Johnson dies on 13 December.
1785	Boswell's *Journal of a Tour to the Hebrides*; *Poetical Works*, ed. George Kearsley.
1786	Thrale-Piozzi's *Anecdotes of the Late Samuel Johnson*.
1787	*The Works of Samuel Johnson*, ed. John Hawkins; Volume I is his *Life of Johnson*.
1791	Boswell's *Life of Samuel Johnson, LL.D.*

Abbreviations

Bibliography	J. D. Fleeman, *A Bibliography of the Works of Samuel Johnson: Treating His Published Works from the Beginnings to 1984*, 2 vols. (Oxford: Clarendon Press, 2000)
Journey	Samuel Johnson, *A Journey to the Western Islands of Scotland*, ed. J. D. Fleeman (Oxford: Clarendon Press, 1985)
LAEP	*The Complete Poems of Samuel Johnson*, ed. Robert D. Brown and Robert DeMaria, Jr, Longman's Annotated English Poets series (London: Routledge, 2024)
Letters	*The Letters of Samuel Johnson*, ed. Bruce Redford, 5 vols. (Oxford: Clarendon Press, 1992–4)
Life	James Boswell, *The Life of Samuel Johnson, LL.D.*, ed. G. B. Hill, rev. L. F. Powell, 6 vols. (Oxford: Clarendon Press, 1934–64)
Lives	Samuel Johnson, *The Lives of the Most Eminent English Poets: With Critical Observations on Their Works*, ed. Roger Lonsdale, 4 vols. (Oxford University Press, 2006)
Miscellanies	G. B. Hill, ed., *Johnsonian Miscellanies*, 2 vols. (Oxford: Clarendon Press, 1897)
Works	Robert DeMaria, Jr, Allen T. Hazen, John H. Middendorf, et al., *The Yale Edition of the Works of Samuel Johnson*, 23 vols. (New Haven, CT: Yale University Press, 1958-2019)

Biblical citations are from the King James Version. *Dictionary* quotations, unless otherwise stated, are from the 1755 edition.

Chapter 1

Life and Times

> To judge rightly of an author we must transport ourselves to his time, and examine what were the wants of his contemporaries, and what were his means of supplying them.
> (*Lives*, II.119)

Samuel Johnson's last great work, his *Prefaces Critical and Biographical* to *The Lives of the Poets*, has – like so much of his writing – a strong autobiographical element. In these short biographies of English poets, begun in the late 1770s, Johnson also reviews his own life – as an author, a keen observer, and an important actor in the literary world of the eighteenth century. When the course of writing his *Prefaces* brings him to Joseph Addison (1672–1719), Johnson feels that he has entered the period of time that he himself inhabited. He writes, with an allusion to Horace, 'I begin to feel myself *walking upon ashes under which the fire is not extinguished*' (*Lives*, III.18). Johnson felt a particular affinity with Addison: both attended Lichfield Grammar School, and Addison's literary career served as a model for Johnson's. Both writers combined journalism with ambitious works of verse drama, poetry, and travel writing. Johnson was, as he wrote about Addison, describing the beginning of his own era. What was for Johnson the age of Addison would gradually become in his maturity the age of Johnson.

The World Johnson Was Born Into

When Johnson was born, on 18 September 1709, Addison and Richard Steele's (1671–1729) *Tatler* essays were just starting to make their presence felt. Alexander Pope (1688–1744) was an astonishing newcomer on the scene, writing his precocious pastoral poems and about to begin work on his translation of Homer, which Johnson considered so important to the literary world. In 1709, Jonathan Swift (1667–1745) was still good friends with the Whigs Addison and Steele, though he would soon join the Tory ministry as one of its chief propagandists. Queen Anne – to whom the infant Johnson was brought to be 'touched' as protection against the 'King's Evil' (i.e. scrofula or tuberculosis of the lymph glands) – would reign for five more years, before dying in 1714 and making way for George I and the Hanoverians who still rule today. That the succession passed over the Catholic son of James II, according to the Act of Settlement (1701), remained a sore point for many Britons throughout Johnson's lifetime; Johnson saw the case against the Act of Settlement and had some sympathy with opposition in general but was never affiliated with Jacobites – or, really, with any particular faction.

Johnson's parents, Michael (1656–1731) and Sarah (1669–1759), were relatively old when Samuel was born, and through them, particularly through his father, Johnson could reach back into history. In his *Lives*, Johnson uses some of his father's anecdotes on the trade to extend his account of the publishing industry into the seventeenth century, recalling through him, for example, the great success of John Dryden's poem about King Charles II and the Exclusion Crisis in 1672, *Absalom and Achitophel*. It was, however, the literary world dominated by Pope, Addison, and Swift into which Johnson was born. The English recorded in Johnson's *Dictionary*, for instance, is that written by authors from Shakespeare to Pope and Swift.

If Addison, Pope, and Swift more or less defined the literary and linguistic present for Johnson, his political present was the beginning of the Hanoverian reign, including the administrations of Robert Walpole (1722–42), when the conflict between city and country interests solidified as a contest between Whigs and Tories. Johnson's politics shifted a good deal during his lifetime, but he was culturally Toryish: monarchical, high church, concerned with maintaining social order; against foreign wars and the over-extension of the empire; in favour of concentrating on domestic issues; and supportive of the right of individuals, including authors, to ply their trades and move up in the world without being accused of insubordination.

Melancholy Christianity

Like his politics, Johnson's religion was also fundamentally consistent throughout his life, though not without vicissitudes. A story – probably apocryphal but indicative of Johnson's reputation – relates that his father carried him on his shoulders to hear the charismatic Henry Sacheverell deliver a sermon on his favourite subject, 'The Church in Danger' (i.e. from subversive Whig policies like the toleration of Protestant dissenters). Johnson was a strong churchman and seems to have adhered to the tenets of Church of England bishops such as John Tillotson and Robert South, both of whom he quotes extensively in his

Dictionary. His religion had a strong emphasis on piety and everyday morality, as opposed to theological complexity. The *Dictionary*, for example, is filled with works of practical devotion such as William Wake's *Preparation for Death* and Richard Allestree's *Government of the Tongue*. Even Tillotson and South, for that matter, are relatively practical in their approach to religion.

Henry Hammond's *Of Fundamentals*, also much quoted in the *Dictionary*, provides a clue to Johnson's theology in its emphasis on the beliefs in which all Christians can concur. For Hammond, as for Johnson, attaining Heaven is less about correct belief and more about putting Christian ethics into practice. Johnson's belief in the importance of financial generosity – to give one example – is evident throughout his life. It appears not only in the stories popularized by Boswell in which Johnson empties his pockets in alms for the poor, but also in his interest throughout the *Lives of the Poets* in rehearsing his subjects' records of charitable giving. Richard Savage, reprehensibly mendacious in so many ways, earns something like sainthood in Johnson's account because he shares his meagre wealth with the destitute woman who gave evidence against him in his murder trial (*Lives*, III.137–8).

There were, of course, plenty of religious views that Johnson found beyond the pale. He was particularly hard on religious enthusiasm, which he defined in the *Dictionary* as 'A vain belief of private revelation; a vain confidence of divine favour or communication.' He would have been thinking of sects such as the Muggletonians, who laid claims to the thrill of prophecy from the time of the Interregnum on. Johnson, by contrast, was careful in his prayers and meditations to confess his ignorance of divine matters. When he prayed for the soul of his departed wife, for example, he always did so 'conditionally', as he would not presume to know enough about the afterlife to be sure such prayers could have any effect.

Nevertheless, Johnson was somewhat affected by the evangelicalism that swept through the Midlands in his youth. He disagreed with its tenets, perhaps, but he absorbed some of its attitudes. He was not a follower of the inner light, but he believed (later in life, at least) in the power of grace extended directly by God (through the agency of Christ) to individuals prepared to receive it. His letters to Hill Boothby (1708–56) indicate his disagreement with her evangelicalism, but his interest in marrying her testifies to his tolerance of her views. In his last prayer, he uses the Protestant language of 'conversion' to describe his preparation for death (*Works*, I.417–18).

Whatever Johnson's religious opinions – and it is difficult to know them for sure – throughout his life he was dogged by religious melancholy of a kind that is more closely associated with Protestant sects such as Methodism and even Moravianism, with which Johnson's friend John Wesley was briefly associated, than with high church doctrine. Johnson was frightened of damnation, as his famous exchange with Dr Adams, master of Pembroke College in 1784, shows:

> The amiable Dr. Adams suggested that God was infinitely good. JOHNSON. 'That he is infinitely good, as far as the perfection of his nature will allow, I certainly believe; but it is necessary for good upon the whole, that individuals should be punished. As to an *individual*, therefore, he is not infinitely good; and as I cannot be *sure* that I have fulfilled the conditions on which salvation is granted, I am afraid I may be one of those who shall be damned.' (looking dismally.) DR. ADAMS. 'What do you mean by damned?' JOHNSON, (passionately and loudly) 'Sent to Hell, Sir, and punished everlastingly.' (*Life*, IV.299)

G. B. Hill links this passage to *Rambler* 110, where Johnson describes a sinful man as 'suspended over the abyss of eternal perdition' (*Works*, IV.224). Such hellfire and brimstone is conspicuous in some high church works, such as the sermons of Jeremy Taylor, but it also abounds in evangelical divines: the American Jonathan Edwards, who spoke of man as a 'spider' 'in the hands of an angry God', as well as in the works of John Bunyan. *Pilgrim's Progress* was among Johnson's favourite books, and it seems likely that the bipolar, staccato rhythm of hope and fear in Bunyan's works (especially *Grace Abounding*) was familiar to him. The high church, on the other hand, regarded religious melancholy as a kind of failing and preached a sort of confidence that Johnson could not achieve, although he often berated himself for his failure to do so – for, in other words, entertaining 'vain scruples' instead of grooming his faith to perfection.

Johnson identified with other people who suffered from religious scruples and religious melancholy. When he heard that Christopher Smart had been confined to a madhouse, he told Charles Burney, 'I did not think he ought to be shut up. His infirmities were not noxious to society. He insisted on people praying with him; and I'd as lief pray with Kit Smart as any one else. Another charge was, that he did not love clean linen; and I have no passion for it' (*Life*, I.397). Johnson sometimes asked people to pray with him or suddenly began to pray himself, and when he was talking to himself, he was 'frequently uttering pious ejaculations' and prayers (*Life* I.483, V.307; *Miscellanies*, II.273). Like Smart, William Collins suffered from mental disease with religious overtones, and Johnson sympathized deeply. He wrote to Joseph Warton when Collins was discharged from an asylum but still 'weak and low': 'Poor dear Collins ... I have often been near his state' (*Letters*, I.91 and n. 1).

It may be that mental disease – melancholy, as it was usually called in the eighteenth century – takes a religious form for a person concerned with religion, and Johnson, like most intellectuals of his time, was intensely concerned with religion. His melancholy presented itself in other dimensions of his thinking and acting as well, and that from a very early age. In fact, his melancholy may well have had a physical cause. His birth was evidently difficult; he contracted scrofula as an infant and suffered scars from the brutal treatment of the time, which involved making suppurating incisions on his neck. His eyesight was poor all his life: he was near-sighted, and it seems likely that his left eye wandered and may have been useless. He also had tics and spasms of the sort now associated with Tourette's Syndrome, and his hands were chronically cramped, as at least two of Joshua Reynolds's portraits indicate (1756 and 1765).

Johnson's Mind

As the modern diagnosis of Tourette's suggests, Johnson's physical ills were associated with psychological problems. He suffered from melancholy and in particular what is now called obsessive-compulsive disorder. He compulsively performed ritual movements such as touching or stepping on certain places on entering or leaving his house, and he endured obsessive intrusive thoughts of a sexual and perhaps violent nature. He berated himself for having such thoughts in his diaries, many of which he destroyed before his death. As a teenager, he sent a description of his symptoms to his uncle Swynfen, a doctor in Birmingham. He was so alarmed to find that his uncle had discussed these symptoms with others that he never spoke to him again.

In addition to his physical and psychological ills, however, Johnson was also born with extraordinary intellectual gifts. He had a highly retentive mind from an early age and could memorize poetry and religious lessons with remarkable speed. He probably did not write the epitaph of a duckling on whom he carelessly trod at the age of three or five, as family lore held (*LAEP*, 805), but by fifteen he was writing polished if mainly derivative verse. His childhood friend Edmund Hector reports that he helped other grammar school students with their work so often that he was sometimes carried to school as a hero (*Life*, I.47). His diaries indicate that he was somewhat contemptuous of his immediate family: he found his mother dull-witted and his father merely mercantile, and he was distressed by their quarrelling. He also looked down on his brother Nathaniel, a more gregarious, risk-taking young man who sadly got into debt and probably took his own life. In later life, Johnson never stopped thinking about his family with guilt; one of his last acts was to arrange for a commemorative stone to be laid for them in St Michael's Church in Lichfield (*Works*, XIX.523–4).

Contemptuous of mere shopkeeping, even when the shop was a relatively high-toned bookstore, Johnson felt himself drawn away from Market Street, where the family house and shop were built, towards the higher society of the Cathedral Close, especially at the house called the 'Bishop's Palace', the residence of the barrister Gilbert Walmesley. There, Johnson met prominent local Whigs and began an argument about Milton that he would continue on and off for his entire life. In 1725, at the age of sixteen, Johnson stepped into more elevated society when he visited his cousin Cornelius Ford at Pedmore near Stourbridge. He had studied with the estimable, if 'very severe', Reverend John Hunter at Lichfield Grammar (*Life*, I.44), but in Ford he found a teacher who at thirty-one had already been a Cambridge don and an associate of literary lights such as Alexander Pope. The visit, which was planned as a six-week holiday, became a six-month sojourn that had a lasting effect on Johnson. Ford was known not only for learning and literate society, but also for dissipation: he is purportedly the louche parson in Hogarth's satirical print *A Modern Midnight Conversation*. Fifty years after his visit to Pedmore, Johnson paid tribute to Ford in his 'Life' of the poet John Fenton, lamenting his dissolute ways but praising his abilities, which 'might have enabled him to excel among the virtuous and the wise' (*Lives*, III.91).

After six months at Pedmore, Johnson was refused readmission to Lichfield Grammar School and placed at Stourbridge, thus extending his stay in that neighbourhood to a full year. During this time, Johnson wrote most of his extant juvenilia, including the first of many attempts at translating Horace's *Odes*.

When he returned to Lichfield in 1726, Johnson was again in company with Walmesley – a man he would later praise for his 'amplitude of learning' and 'copiousness of communication' ('Life of Smith', *Lives*, II.179), and who was certainly among those whom Johnson said he 'wished to please' but were 'sunk into the grave' when he published his *Dictionary* in 1755 (*Works*, XVIII.113). During this period, Johnson continued his study of the classics on his own, fell into a fruitless infatuation with Edmund Hector's sister, wrote some love poetry, and prepared for longer flight to Oxford.

A Disappointing Education

Johnson's thirteen months at Oxford University began after Michaelmas (29 September) in 1729. In Cornelius Ford and Gilbert Walmesley, Johnson had found father figures whom he wished to emulate more than Michael Johnson the provincial bookseller. Unfortunately, he did not find another such figure at Oxford. What he found instead was a caste system that valued social status more than learning. Indignant and rebellious, he disdained his tutor, William Jorden, and famously reported that he had been fined twopence for sliding on the ice in Christ Church Meadow when he was supposed to be at a lecture not worth a penny. He refused to write a mandatory exercise on the Gunpowder Plot and instead wrote an elaborate, learned excuse called 'Somnium' in imitation of Macrobius, a Latin satirist too obscure to be in the curriculum at Oxford.

On one occasion, he was overheard muttering to himself about leaving Oxford: 'Well, I have a mind to see what is done in other places of learning. I'll go and visit the Universities abroad. I'll go to France and Italy. I'll go to Padua' (*Life*, I.73; Johnson did eventually, forty-six years later, set foot in France, but, to his sorrow, he never got to Italy). His experience at Oxford was largely negative, and it may have stimulated some powerfully oppositional energy. Johnson wrote a Latin translation of Pope's *Messiah* for a college collection called *A Miscellany of Poems by Several Hands* (1731). This is the only Latin poem in the collection, and, in a way, Johnson was both challenging his fellow students academically and aligning himself with a great writer whose Roman Catholicism had barred him from matriculation at Oxford. Johnson was not a crypto-Catholic, despite refusing the Gunpowder Plot exercise and imitating Pope, but he was an outsider at Oxford, and he may have expressed that in his first published work.

Johnson's most important poem from this period, 'The Young Author', also aligned him with writers in the world outside of the academy:

> So the young author panting for a name,
> And fir'd with pleasing hope of endless fame,
> Intrusts his happiness to human kind,
> More false, more cruel than the seas and wind.
>
> (lines 11–14)

This prefigures elements of both *London* and *The Vanity of Human Wishes*, his most important poems. In the *Vanity*, a student is told unceremoniously and ironically to 'pause awhile from letters, to be wise' (line 158).

New Beginnings

When Johnson went home from Oxford over Christmas in 1730, he found his father ill and his financial resources dried up. The fact that he left his books in

Oxford suggests that he was planning to return, but he did not. Michael Johnson died about a year later, and Johnson was faced with making a living. He tried teaching with mixed results: the one position that he secured, at Market Bosworth, was unbearable after six months. After failing to find another teaching job, he went off to Birmingham in 1732 to pursue a career as a journalist. He first wrote essays for *The Birmingham Journal*, edited by Thomas Warren. Whatever he published there is unfortunately lost, but Warren soon commissioned Johnson to write a translation of the Jesuit Father Lobo's *Itinerario*, a Portuguese narrative describing a missionary trip to Abyssinia. Johnson made his translation from the French translation of Lobo's manuscript by Joachim Le Grand, *Relation historique d'Abissinie* (1728). As well as the fee of five guineas, the work had the added benefit of allowing him to hone an approach to literary daywork that he would employ throughout his career. Without straying very far from strict translation, Johnson infuses his work with small digressions on some of his favourite humanistic topics: the vanity of human wishes, the prevalence of ignorance and error, the cruelty of colonial imperialism, and the mendacity of religious excuses for securing financial advantages. In this exercise, Johnson also packed away a good deal of learning about the Middle Eastern world that would serve him well in writing his 'oriental tales', including his novel *Rasselas* and his play *Irene*.

Although he needed daywork, Johnson was still hoping to progress as a serious scholar. In 1734, he borrowed a copy of the works of Angelo Poliziano (1454–94) and put together a proposal for an edition of his Latin poetry. Unsurprisingly, there were few takers in the Midlands, and Johnson began to train his eyes on the metropolis. Under an assumed name, he wrote a letter to Edward Cave, the proprietor of the *Gentleman's Magazine*, offering to raise the tone of that publication with learned contributions, provided 'on reasonable terms' (*Letters*, I.6). The letter did not yield immediate results, but it was the beginning of Johnson's relationship with the London publishers, who would provide the lifeblood of his whole career.

Another of Johnson's proposals was more successful than either his notes on Poliziano or his offer to Cave. He proposed marriage to the widow of Harry Porter, the former Elizabeth Jervis. Tetty, the nickname by which she became known in the Johnsonian world, was twenty years his senior. Her sons rejected the attachment and refused to have anything to do with Johnson. Her daughter Lucy, however, then nineteen, became a lifelong friend. Johnson was suspected of coveting Elizabeth's £600 inheritance, but he told a friend, 'It was a love-marriage upon both sides' (*Life*, I.96). She called him 'the most sensible [i.e. sensitive] man that I ever saw in my life' (*Life*, I.95–6). It is not hard to imagine that Johnson, beset by chronic melancholy, unsure of his path in life, and inexperienced, would find comfort and love with an older woman, and that she, recently bereft, would love a sensitive, highly intelligent young man who understood emotional pain.

With the backing of his wife's money, Johnson set up a school at Edial just outside of Lichfield in a grand old house. He placed an advertisement in the *Gentleman's Magazine* for June 1736: 'At Edial, near *Litchfield* in *Staffordshire*, Young Gentlemen are Boarded, and Taught the *Latin* and *Greek* Languages, by SAMUEL JOHNSON.' The school was not a success – it never attracted more than a handful of students – but Johnson used his free time to make another attempt at authorship. Knowing that playwriting could sometimes provide a fast track to success, he began writing a verse tragedy called *Irene*. His identification with the humanist tradition evident in his proposals for Poliziano also came through in this work, which he set at the fall of Constantinople (1453), then considered the decisive moment in the spread of classical learning in the West. A principal character in Johnson's play is Constantine Lascaris, a Byzantine scholar who fled the occupation of Constantinople and became an influential Greek teacher in Milan and Sicily.

On 2 March 1737, Johnson packed up his manuscript of *Irene*, abandoned his failing school at Edial, and set off for London with the liveliest of his few students, David Garrick. Three days after their departure, Johnson's brother Nathaniel was buried in St Michael's Church beside his father. He was twenty-four and possibly died by suicide, though his grave being in sacred ground argues against that assumption. It is unclear when Johnson received the news, but it was at about the same time that Garrick learned his father had died. The two nevertheless persevered and completed the 125-mile trip to the city in around ten days, alternately walking and riding a packhorse. They made an odd pair: Johnson was, according to his friend Hester Thrale, just under six feet (very tall for the time), while Garrick was closer to five feet.

Johnson's most important connection in London was Edward Cave. On 12 July 1737, Johnson wrote to Cave proposing a translation of Paolo Sarpi's *History of the Council of Trent* (1619). This was to be a serious contribution to intellectual history and a subtly patriotic statement in support of the Church of England: as a Venetian statesman, Sarpi had famously resisted the power of the pope over the free state of Venice.

Cave's resources were so tied up in 1738 that it took a year for him to publish Johnson's proposals and a life of Sarpi. (Publishing, especially in the days of cold type and very expensive paper, was a capital-intensive business.) The project as a whole foundered after this delay because it transpired that another translator – also, oddly, named Johnson – was at work on the same project. Despite its failure in itself, the Sarpi project had the important effect of inaugurating Johnson's work as a biographer: it was the first of nearly seventy he wrote over the course of his career. The Sarpi project also ushered Johnson into the world of Cave's *Gentleman's Magazine* (see Chapter 2).

Building a Career

At the beginning of this period of Johnson's heaviest involvement with the *Gentleman's Magazine*, Cave published *London*, Johnson's second most important poem after *The Vanity of Human Wishes*. As an imitation of a satire by the Roman poet Juvenal, *London* kept up Johnson's pretensions to a life of scholarship, while also situating him on the contemporary scene. The politics of the poem are 'patriotic' (i.e. anti-Walpolian), but the figures who speak are authors, and Johnson as ever identifies himself with that class, rather than with politicians of any stripe.

At about the same time, Johnson produced two fiercely anti-Walpole tracts: *Marmor Norfolciense* (1739) and *A Compleat Vindication of the Licensers of the Stage* (1739). These are satirical works that channel the irony and savage indignation of Swift, who was still alive, but they did not lead Johnson to take a durable, partisan position in politics.

In the five years between 1738 and 1743, Johnson was extremely busy as a writer, but in 1739 he found time for a trip to Lichfield and environs to settle some family business and socialize with old friends. Tetty, significantly, did not join him: the marriage had hit a rough patch. When he returned to London, Johnson continued to build a career. He got to know some wealthy publishers, as well as fellow hacks in the literary-journalistic world known as 'Grub Street'. One important connection was Thomas Birch, a hub of communication in the Grub Street world and the author-editor of an immense biographical dictionary. Birch was in correspondence with potential literary patrons, such as Lord Hardwicke and Lord Orrery; with booksellers such as Robert Dodsley and William Strahan; with their trade publishers or distributors, such as Mary Cooper and James Crokatt; with writers such as Richard Savage and Alexander Pope; and with literary workers further down the food chain who were sometimes reduced to translating and indexing, such as George Psalmanazaar and William Guthrie. Johnson acted as a kind of chaperone for dinners with Birch and Elizabeth Carter, whom Birch wooed as a potential wife. (Carter was finally appalled by his advances and left London for her father's home in Deal.)

Birch tried unsuccessfully to get Johnson's play *Irene* produced and published, beginning no later than 1741. In the end, however, it was Garrick who promoted that project for Johnson – but not until 1749. By then, a great deal more had happened in Johnson's career. He had gradually reduced his commitment to the *Gentleman's Magazine* after taking a large commission to prepare a catalogue for the sale of the printed books in the magnificent Harleian Library. The catalogue, the first of its kind to command a price in the bookshops, began publication in 1743 and ran to five volumes. Johnson worked with William Oldys, the Harleian librarian and a well-established bibliographer; it is likely that Johnson received part of his pay in books because otherwise it is hard to imagine how such expensive volumes as George Hickes's massive *Thesaurus* wound up in his own private library.

In August 1743, one of Johnson's and Birch's most notable mutual contacts died and instantly became a hot topic for biography. Richard Savage had walked the streets of London with Johnson; together they had heard the chimes at midnight. He was therefore an obvious choice to write Savage's storied life. There had been biographical accounts before his death, but now the whole story could be told, and Johnson was in a position to tell it. He got fifteen guineas for the job from Cave on 14 December and by 11 February 1744 the work of 186 pages was published. Johnson could always write quickly. *An Account of the Life of Mr. Richard Savage* was not a best-seller (there wasn't a second edition until 1748), but it was a work of great interest to the Grub Street world and helped put Johnson on the map for London publishers. Johnson's biography is a rather tendentious apology for Savage, blaming his putative mother (who was probably not related to him) for much of his depravity, but it is a great read. It shows Johnson clearly emerged from his shell of classical learning and willing to perform for a general audience. Joshua Reynolds famously took up the book while leaning on a fireplace mantle and couldn't put it down until he had finished and his book-holding arm was dead numb (*Life*, I.165).

In 1745, Johnson got his first commission that involved, eventually, a group of London publishers instead of a single 'patron' like Cave. His proposals for an edition of Shakespeare, which included notes on *Macbeth* as a specimen, were published by Cave; but by the time Johnson's edition, *The Plays of William Shakespeare*, eventually came out in eight volumes in 1765, there were eleven publishers (or booksellers, as they were then called) on the title page.

Gough Square

In 1745, Robert Dodsley engaged Johnson to help with his two-volume self-schooling text, *The Preceptor*. Johnson wrote the introduction and one of the concluding allegories, 'The Vision of Theodore, the Hermit of Teneriffe'. Johnson's 'Vision' is one of the most concentrated statements of his educational and moral philosophy and, he said, his own favourite among his works. In the allegory, the pilgrims' ascent to the mountaintop of existence is aided by education and reason, but only religion can lead them to true happiness. The enemies of the pilgrims' ascent are bad habits, indolence, ambition, and avarice. Like so much of Johnson's writing, 'The Vision of Theodore' is fundamentally a performance on the theme of Ecclesiastes 1.14, 'All is vanity'. But the work was not in vain for Johnson's career.

Dodsley was a self-made man who had forced his way to the forefront of London publishing partly by hitching his wagon to a star, in the diminutive form of Alexander Pope. After Pope's death in 1744, Dodsley needed a new lead horse, and he chose well in harnessing Johnson. He knew Johnson through Birch and through his main distributor, or trade publisher, Mary Cooper. The *Account of the Life of Richard Savage* showed that Johnson could write popular prose rooted in classical learning and age-old tropes. The 'Hermit of Teneriffe' confirmed it.

In 1746, Dodsley brought many of his fellow London booksellers together around a plan to publish *A Dictionary of the English Language* by Samuel Johnson. Johnson wrote his 'Short Scheme for compiling a new Dictionary', and the contract was signed on 18 June. The booksellers agreed to pay Johnson £1,575, a vast sum (five years' worth of the pension he was ultimately to receive in 1762). Nevertheless, Johnson ran through the money in three years: the expenses involved in making the *Dictionary* were great, and Johnson was never frugal. By 1749, he had leased a grand house in Gough Square, just off the Strand, and he would end up staying there for ten years; it is still 'Dr Johnson's House'. Then, he hired a total of six secretaries, or amanuenses, to help with preparing the copy, and he had to supply them with paper (always expensive), pens, and ink. He needed furniture for his workers, books, and probably victuals as well, but the house was the main thing. When he ran out of money, Johnson sought supplementary income from other projects and further payments from the publishers.

The Gough Square house provided not only the workspace (the garret) in which the *Dictionary* was composed, but also a nesting place for the odd collection of souls who made up Johnson's household and his primary domestic society for the rest of his life. He met Robert Levet in 1746 and sheltered this largely self-taught, poor doctor in his home, with some gaps, until his death in 1783. In 1748, Johnson allowed Anna Williams, the daughter of an experimenter in electricity, to undergo an operation for cataracts in his capacious house. The operation failed; Anna became blind; and Johnson took her in as a dependant for virtually the rest of her life. During his wife's long illness and her residence in Hampstead, Johnson hired Elizabeth Desmoulins (née Swynfen) to assist her. This woman, the daughter of Johnson's godfather, became an inmate of Johnson's house in the 1770s.

There were others, including Polly Carmichael, who may have been a reformed prostitute, but most notable of all was Francis Barber, a Jamaican child born into slavery on the plantation of Colonel Bathurst and transported to London when the plantation, along with the rest of the enslaved people, was sold. Barber was first in the custody of the colonel's son Richard, a good friend of Johnson's, and then remanded to Johnson's care when he was about seven. Barber gained his legal freedom on the death of his former master; served Johnson as household help; got an education with Johnson's assistance; went to sea with the navy briefly; and eventually returned to marry and live with Johnson, with his wife and child. The relationship matured into one of familial devotion, and Barber became Johnson's heir.[1]

By the time he began the *Dictionary*, Johnson's marriage had been largely upended by Elizabeth's worsening physical condition. As Johnson's only extant letter to her shows, she hurt her leg in London while Johnson was on his six-month-long visit to the Midlands from August 1739 to March 1740. The letter is very tender and marked with homely Midlands usages that are absent in Johnson's other correspondence. Johnson addresses Tetty as 'thee', for example. It is likely, however, that Johnson's long absence was a sign of marital trouble. It is also likely that the treatment for Tetty's injury included opiates and that she compounded the effect of these with alcohol. Reports from Johnson's friends of her flushed complexion and excessive make-up, as well as some derisive comments about her state of mind, suggest Tetty was not doing well in London. By the mid-1740s she was spending a lot of time out of the city (mostly in Hampstead) for her health, while Johnson stayed in town, working hard and keeping up with his contacts as a professional writer must.

Johnson published his *Plan of a Dictionary*, dedicated to Lord Chesterfield, in 1747, but soon – even before all the sheets of the first issue were printed – Johnson regretted his approach to the great man and expunged his name and titles from the heading of his work. Chesterfield was not, as Johnson realized, willing to support the project: instead, he wrote two articles in *The World* in 1754 touting its imminent appearance and implying that he had fostered the project in some way. Johnson responded on 7 February 1755, two months before the publication of the *Dictionary* on 15 April, with an indignant letter: 'The notice which you have been pleased to take of my Labours, had it been early, had been kind; but it has been delayed till I am indifferent and cannot enjoy it, till I am solitary and cannot impart it, till I am known and do not want [i.e. need] it' (*Letters*, I.96).

Johnson also asked Chesterfield: 'Is not a Patron, My Lord, one who looks with unconcern on a Man struggling for Life in the water and when he has reached ground encumbers him with help.' This passage especially has been reasonably interpreted as a declaration of independence on the part of authors from the patronage system in the arts, a set-up that persisted well into the eighteenth century and made most authors dependent on the benefactions of the wealthy. Certain genres of writing – including journalism of all kinds and playwriting – were sometimes financially viable through direct appeals to the reading public; others, such as poetry, were very rarely so. Those who escaped the need for noble patronage, however, needed the support of the booksellers, who were often ruthless in their exploitation of authors. When Johnson called Robert Dodsley his 'patron' (*Letters*, I.173) – although Dodsley was a publisher rather than an aristocratic benefactor – he was candidly acknowledging his choice to operate in the new economy of authorship. That said, Johnson also tacitly acknowledged the need for old-fashioned patronage – at least for others – by ghostwriting so many dedications to nobles on behalf of his friends.

In 1749, Johnson cashed in on some of his connections to publish his greatest poem, one of the best verse satires in any language, *The Vanity of Human Wishes*. Like *London*, the *Vanity* is an imitation of a satire by Juvenal – this time the expansive and philosophical tenth satire, rather than the sharper, more scurrilous and indignant third. The *Vanity* certainly has political moments – the section on the fall of Wolsey can be read as a celebration of the fall of Walpole, for example – but on the whole it is less particular and less dangerous than *London*. Robert Dodsley was again the publisher, but this time he was also the chief backer: Johnson was fast becoming the lead author in Dodsley's stable of talent.

In the same year, through the influence of Garrick, who had been performing bits of Johnson's play at the end of some of his productions in Drury Lane, Johnson was finally able to publish *Irene* and see it performed in its entirety. Dodsley and Cooper were again the publishers. On the first night, the play was hissed off the stage because of the melodramatic murder scene. With the murder taken off-stage, the play ran for another eight nights, making it at least a moderate success. Johnson netted almost £200, plus £100 from Dodsley for the copyright.

In 1750, after the first three letters of the *Dictionary* were set up in type, work came to a halt. Johnson was probably out of funds, despite his record earnings in 1749. Although beholden to numerous London publishers for copy, he struck a deal with two others to produce an essay twice a week for two years. Those essays, averaging around 1,500 words apiece, would be the sole content of the publication called *The Rambler*, and he would assume the identity of 'Mr Rambler' (see Chapter 2). Johnson published the essays anonymously, but his authorship was an open secret, and he was soon known as Mr Rambler.

Bereavement and Fame

The *Rambler* came to an end on 14 March 1752. The last two numbers are especially gloomy. On 17 March, Elizabeth Johnson had died, sending Johnson into an abyss of melancholy. He wrote prayers of contrition and composed a sermon for her service, intending it to be read by his friend John Taylor; but he did not attend her funeral in Bromley, nine miles south-east of Charing Cross, nor did he ever visit her grave. Taylor did not deliver the sermon, on the grounds that it praised Tetty too highly (*Works*, XIV.261n1). Johnson's sermon suggests his wife was not intellectual, but rather practical and kind:

> her wit was never employed to scoff at goodness, nor her reason to dispute against truth. In this age of wild opinions, she was as free from scepticism as the cloistered virgin. She never wished to signalize herself by the singularity of paradox. She had a just diffidence of her own reason, and desired to practice rather than to dispute . . . She was exact and regular in her devotions . . . grateful for every kindness that she received, and willing to impart assistance of every kind to all whom her little power enabled her to benefit.   (*Works*, XIV.269)

Whether or not Johnson's praise is just, it does not seem overblown for a eulogy. Moreover, it reflects to some extent Johnson's sense of his own moral failings. He was not diffident of his reason, but he was given to scepticism and paradox; and he was beset by scruples and doubts in his religion. He aspired to kindness and generosity but did not always show it. He talked for victory at times rather than truth, and he could blast opponents to such a degree that he was later filled with remorse. If the Tetty he created in the sermon was an ideal, it was one to which he himself aspired.

Thirteen months after Tetty's death, Johnson sought a second wife in Hill Boothby, the daughter of a distinguished Derbyshire gentleman who had been an important customer of Johnson's father. Johnson addressed her in his letters as 'My Sweet Angel' and professed that he loved her. They differed on matters of religion, but the real bar to marriage was Boothby's commitment to care for the orphaned children of a friend; she sustained those duties for only a short time before dying in January 1756, leaving Johnson once more bereft. Though there were many women in his life after 1756, Johnson never sought marriage again.

In 1753, he wrote a prayer before re-engaging with the *Dictionary* and starting the second volume: 'Oh God who hast hitherto supported me enable me to proceed in this labour & in the Whole task of my present state that when I shall render up at the last day an account of the talent committed to me I may receive pardon for the sake of Jesus Christ. Amen' (*Works*, I.50). The great book was at last published officially on 15 April 1755; copies were delivered to the French Académie and to the Accademia della Crusca in Florence. Johnson was hailed in Great Britain and on the Continent. He was famous – as well as broke, sick, and tired. In March, Johnson was briefly under arrest for a debt of less than £6. Samuel Richardson promptly sent him six guineas, but Johnson needed work. Around the same time that Richardson bailed him out, Johnson began editing the *Literary Magazine*, and he signed a contract with Jacob Tonson for a new edition of Shakespeare, the project for which Johnson had originally published proposals in 1745.

Now, he issued new proposals and achieved a column in Tonson's financial ledger, where he was credited with various sums – including £40 in 1758 when he was again under arrest for debt. (Johnson never had his own bank account, unlike Alexander Pope, and existed financially mainly on the ledgers of William Strahan and Robert Dodsley, his publishers.)

The *Literary Magazine* kept Johnson very busy for about thirteen months, during which period he reviewed some thirty-nine books and wrote several other articles. He clearly was not making enough money on this job, but it did give him an avenue for venting his anger over the Seven Years' War. He was particularly moved by the deplorable case of Admiral Byng, who was unfairly sentenced to death in the aftermath of the Spanish victory at Fort Mahon, Menorca. The cruelty exhibited in war – to the enemy as well as to the troops of one's own country – most appalled Johnson. He was against colonial expansion for a host of reasons, including the inevitable weakening of the homeland because of it, but cruelty of any kind angered him. He was against it in war as well as in society with respect to the poor, the disadvantaged, the sick, and the mentally disabled.

In 1758, Johnson, still in need of money, and still angry about the war, agreed to write a regular essay called the *Idler* to be published in the *Universal Magazine*. He carried on once a week for two years. The *Idler* is more topical, generally, than the *Rambler* and less heavily philosophical. It is also more political, inveighing sometimes against the Seven Years' War and sometimes against war in general. One instalment – the original number 22 – was so cynical about warfare that it was rejected from the collected, hard-bound edition. Despite earning a decent income from the *Idler* (three guineas per essay), Johnson did not have the money to handle the expenses incurred by his mother's last illness. He struck up a bargain with William Strahan, and in the evenings of one week produced the two small volumes of *Rasselas*: an oriental tale, his only extended work of fiction, and by all accounts his most popular work. It has never been out of print; there have been over 400 editions; and it has been translated into 50 different languages.

By the time the last *Idler* was published in April 1760, Johnson had been out of his grand house in Gough Square for over a year. He took rooms in several places, finally settling on Inner Temple Lane. He temporarily lost his household of odd fellows, although Francis Barber, just released from the navy, may have stayed with him even in his straitened circumstances. Johnson penned some anti-slavery pieces at this time and a host of other small works: he wrote a preface in support of the Republican Thomas Hollis's appeal for clothing the French prisoners of war; several dedications, prefaces, and proposals for friends, such as Charlotte Lennox and Giuseppe Baretti; a series of letters in support of his friend Thomas Gwynn's design for a bridge with semicircular arches at Blackfriars; letters for the Society of Artists, whose first president would be his friend Joshua Reynolds; proposals for a miscellany ostensibly by Anna Williams; a life of Roger Ascham; and many other odd jobs. His expenses were much reduced, but he was still scraping to get by.

Then, rather suddenly, halfway through 1762, he was granted a civil pension of £300 per year. Since he was known as a long-time critic of the government – from *London* (1738) to his anti-war essays in the *Idler* (1760–2) – he was pilloried in the press for accepting a pension from the crown. There was no use denying the appearance of hypocrisy; he had defined 'pension' in the *Dictionary* as 'pay given to a state hireling for treason to his country'. Rather than fight it out in London, Johnson went on holiday to Devonshire with Joshua Reynolds, who was from Plymouth, and let the press have its way. He was assured by Lord Bute, the prime minister, that the pension was given without any expectation of future service or consideration of past political involvement (*Letters*, I.207–8 and n.6).

With his new-found wealth, Johnson resumed living in quarters ample enough to house his familiar inmates; he chose to live in the fortuitously named Johnson's Court, right around the corner from Gough Square. Relieved of the need for day labour, Johnson got back to work on his long-delayed edition of Shakespeare. He had issued new proposals for the work in 1756, and the subscribers were wondering where the book was. It finally appeared in October of 1765 in eight quarto volumes. Johnson's place in literary history was now firmly established. He had compiled the best dictionary of English and the best edition of the best writer in English. (It is impossible to imagine anyone doing something today that would even remotely resemble this dual achievement.) His edition of Shakespeare, which dovetailed with his *Dictionary* because Shakespeare is so conspicuous in its illustrative quotations, both energized the national exaltation of the Bard, epitomized in the Shakespeare Jubilee of 1769, and gained greater importance through it. Shakespeare was Britain's poet, and Johnson was Shakespeare's (and therefore Britain's) critic and scholar. In addition to the *Dictionary* and Shakespeare, Johnson had written volumes of brilliant essays, an extended work of fiction, and hundreds of other works of all descriptions, and all, or almost all, with characteristic power. It was time to rest from the isolation of literary toil.

Boswell and the Thrales

Johnson's literary career was less isolating than one might assume, because he wrote so much more rapidly than most people, but he craved company. It was just the right time, then, for new friends to arrive in his life, first and foremost in the lively form of James Boswell. They met for the first time on 16 May 1763 in Tom Davies's bookshop. Davies himself was an old actor, and in Boswell's telling of the scene Davies theatrically quotes *Hamlet* – 'Look, my Lord, it comes' – as through a glass door in the back of his shop he spies Johnson approaching. With a kind of psychological prescience, Davies was casting Johnson as the ghost of Boswell's father. 'Don't tell him where I come from', whispers Boswell to Davies, and Davies, who has already spoken Boswell's name, cries, 'From Scotland.' Boswell squeaks, 'I do indeed come from Scotland, but I cannot help it', setting up Johnson to thunder: 'That, Sir, I find, is what a very great many of your countrymen cannot help' (*Life*, I.392). And the two are off, making an odd couple of subject and biographer unsurpassed in English literature. True, Boswell exaggerated their closeness and the amount of time they spent together. That, however, is a testimony to the power and ingenuity of Boswell's writing, which makes his Johnson so fully present and alive that it eclipsed for generations the Johnson who comes across even in his own greatest works.

Early in 1765, probably on 9 January, Johnson made the acquaintance of Hester Lynch Thrale and her husband Henry. After some success as the owner of a brewery, he was seeking to be an MP for Southwark and in other ways to rise above his station. She was a beautiful, intelligent, and accomplished young woman, not yet twenty-three, married a little over a year to a man thirteen years her senior. It was not a love match, and it was full of pain as only four of their twelve children survived into adulthood. Hester was determined, however, to have a circle of intelligent, artistic friends, and she succeeded brilliantly. At the centre of the circle was Johnson, who was given his own room at the Thrale house in Streatham, about seven miles south of Gough Square, now part of Greater London but then a village on a country hill. Johnson also had accommodations at Brighthelmstone (Brighton) where the Thrales had a seaside residence. Johnson wrote more, and more intimate, letters to Hester Thrale than to any other correspondent, and he confided in her all his hopes and fears. Their affection for each other was deep, and when, after the death of her husband in 1780, Hester did the unthinkable and fell in love with her music teacher Gabriele Piozzi, Johnson was devastated. (The second marriage divided all of Hester's friends and relatives, most of whom found her attachment to a Catholic, an Italian, and a near-servant shamefully carnal.)

While the Thrale family was intact, it provided not only a social circle for Johnson but also a means of travel, one of his great unsatisfied desires. He and the Thrales went together to northern Wales to see the ancestral home of the Salusburys – a trip cut short by the calling of a general election – and later to France on Johnson's only voyage outside the British Isles. Johnson kept journals of both trips, but neither amounted to much. The grand trip he planned with the Thrales was to Italy; their mutual friend the Genovese Giuseppe Baretti had it all mapped out, the suitcases were packed and sent ahead, when news came that Harry, the Thrale's eldest boy, had suddenly died. The trip was cancelled, and the idea was never revived.

That was in 1776. In the autumn of 1773, Johnson had taken the longest and most productive journey of his life – a three-month tour of Scotland with Boswell. Both men kept journals, and both produced books about the experience. Johnson's *A Journey to the Western Islands of Scotland* came out in 1775. Boswell held his book back until the year after Johnson's death, 1785, and used it as a kind of specimen and introduction to his full *Life of Dr. Samuel Johnson, LL.D.*, which did not appear until 1791. Johnson's work shows his mind settling into a late phase, in which he achieved a new kind of clarity. Many of his earlier writings had been marked by tendentiousness, prompted as they were by a particular purpose: defending Edward Cave, apologizing for Richard Savage, glorifying the English language and English literary culture, proclaiming the durability of Shakespeare, and so on. That said, the *Journey to the Western Islands* was itself seen as having an axe to grind against the Scots, despite its attempts to be empirical and objective.

Last Projects

Back in London in the mid 1770s, Johnson was certainly writing for a purpose. He produced two more essays in defence of ministerial politics (*The Patriot*, 1775; *Taxation No Tyranny*, 1776); he had written two others before his Scottish trip (*The False Alarm*, 1770; *Thoughts on Falkland's Islands*, 1771). There is an irony in Johnson presenting himself as a defender of the ministry when he had before his pension been frequently in opposition, but his late political writings display some of the essential features also found in his earlier works: a hatred of slavery; a dim view of colonial expansion; cynicism about war; contempt for cruelty in all its forms; and a sharp eye for hypocrisy. His enthusiasm for expressing some of these foundational commitments led the ministry to order the cancellation of several paragraphs in *Taxation No Tyranny* and put an end to his career as a polemicist. He did not turn against the ministry in *Taxation No Tyranny*, but he pressed his points with such rhetorical energy that his handlers feared a backlash. There had been talk at various times of getting Johnson a place in Parliament, but he had such confidence in his rhetorical powers and took such pleasure in displaying them that he would have been hard for any political leader to manage.

By 1779, the real value of Johnson's pension had been reduced by inflation, and he was casting about for other sources of income. He tried unsuccessfully to get additional funds and to secure a grace-and-favour apartment from the Lord Chamberlain. He did, however, still have credit with the booksellers of London, who engaged him on one more vast project.

Motivated by challenges to what they regarded as their copyrights in English literature, a group of London publishers conceived of a large collection of English poetry running from Cowley and Milton all the way to Gray and Lyttelton – a total of fifty-eight octavo volumes. Johnson's job was to write *Prefaces Critical and Biographical* to the collection. His work swelled over the two years in which he wrote and eventually became a stand-alone set of four octavo volumes called *The Lives of the Poets* (1781). The increased candour and bluntness visible in his *Journey to the Western Islands* is more fully on display in this, his last great work. Part of being frank and plain-spoken for Johnson was drawing material primarily from his own experience. The *Journey* reflects what he saw and not what one was supposed to see. Likewise, the *Lives of the Poets* tells of Johnson's reactions to the English poetry he had been reading for most of his life and not what one could be presumed to say about it. He presents his critical views in an unvarnished way, and he provides his personal, frank opinions about the poets themselves. In doing so, Johnson is necessarily talking about poetry in general and mankind in general; he has ideas about the nature of poetry and the nature of life, but his experience is the foundation of what he says, and some of his autobiography infuses the criticism, as we suggested at the beginning of this chapter. In effect his own sensibility – both aesthetic and moral – becomes the subject of his work. At times, he may rejoice 'to concur with the common reader', as though devoid of critical prejudices (*Lives*, IV.184), and he is partly such a reader; but he is also unique, and his particular point of view is what steadily informs his judgements and makes them so durable and memorable (see Chapter 5).

The End – and After

Johnson remained active in his last years, though he was beset by illness more often and more violently than earlier in life. Gout, a painful sarcocele (a testicular tumour), pulmonary edema, congestive heart failure, and a good deal of pain drove him to take opium and other palliatives – all recorded in his diaries and in his letters to Hester Thrale. His doctors became a significant part of his company, but he kept up with other old friends and made new friends almost to the end. Many of his last writings were for friends, the last of all a dedication that he wrote for Charles Burney's *Account of the Musical Performance ... in commemoration of Handel* (published in 1785, after Johnson's death). His household thinned out. He lost Robert Levet and wrote a moving elegy in his honour, beginning with a sense of his increasing loneliness:

> Condemn'd to Hope's delusive mine,
> As on we toil from day to day,
> By sudden blast, or slow decline,
> Our social comforts drop away.
>
> (lines 1–4)

His other very old companion Anna Williams slipped away near the end of Johnson's life, but Francis Barber survived Johnson as his heir, and many friends memorialized Johnson, collecting anecdotes and biographical details and contributing to Boswell's attempt to preserve Johnson in full and 'Johnsonize' the land.

As he neared the end, Johnson stopped taking opium because he wanted to meet his maker with a clear head. He prepared for his judgement day with prayers, the last of which asks to be forgiven for his 'late conversion' – a clause excised by the scrupulous divinity student George Strahan, in whose care

Johnson left his written prayers. The words evidently suggested to Strahan that Johnson had become a Catholic or experienced some sort of evangelical conversion that put his high church Anglicanism in doubt. Johnson's biographers and acolytes have wanted him to be monumental, monotonal, and fixed in his thinking. But despite his firm ethical commitments, he was versatile, changeable, and sceptical to the end.

Starting in 1785, within months of his death the previous December, an outpouring of works by and about Johnson filled the presses. Short biographies began appearing that year; in 1787, there was a longer one by Sir John Hawkins, a nearly lifelong friend, which served as volume I of the first edition of Johnson's collected works. The *Life* and the *Works* were augmented in the following few years and reprinted and re-edited scores of times over the years. In 1791, Boswell's great *Life* appeared and initiated a competing stream of Johnsoniana that was also reprinted and augmented over the years. Since Johnson's death, there have been only two years in which works of his were not reprinted or re-edited, both war years. It is fair to say that Johnson's afterlife has been as rich and as conspicuous a part of British culture as his life itself (see Chapter 8). Many great scholars on both sides of the Atlantic have dedicated their professional lives to editing and recording the publication of his works, and many more have devoted themselves to interpreting and reinterpreting his writing.

This *Introduction* to Johnson is a further attempt to bring attention to Johnson's works, not as monuments in the history of English literature but as writings that challenge one to read carefully and, just as importantly, to think carefully. 'Clear your *mind* of cant', Johnson urged Boswell (*Life*, IV.221): that is, think for yourself; look at the facts; go to the source; don't passively accept received or modish wisdom. Striking up a relationship with Johnson's works challenges almost every reader to become more intelligent and thoughtful – and, as Johnson entitled one of his most personal poems, to 'know thyself' (*LAEP* 448).

Chapter 2

Journalist

> He may therefore be justly numbered among the benefactors of mankind, who contracts the great rules of life into short sentences, that may be easily impressed on the memory, and taught by frequent recollection to recur habitually to the mind.
> (*Rambler* 175, *Works*, V.160)

In the spring of 1737, the twenty-seven-year-old Johnson arrived in London, carrying with him an unfinished play and a little cash ('two-pence halfpenny', he later claimed, probably a playful exaggeration).[1] One of the places he most wanted to see was St John's Gate in Clerkenwell, the home of the *Gentleman's Magazine* (*GM*). A thriving publication, it was a potential source of work. But to Johnson, the magazine also represented the London literary world in all its energetic diversity. Readers would find in its pages the latest discussions of politics, foreign affairs, economics, literature, science, the domestic arts, and everything else. The contents were advertised on the front page, beneath a large picture of St John's Gate itself. When Johnson first looked at the building, he later said, he 'beheld it with reverence'. There he formed many of the principles which defined his later work.

Reverence might seem a curious emotion for what was, first and foremost, a clever piece of business. The publisher, Edward Cave, had founded the *GM* in 1731 as a monthly collection of extracts from other publications. Nobody had tried this before – indeed, nobody had previously used the word 'magazine' in this sense. Later, it would publish its own articles, but at the start it was a collection of extracts from elsewhere, on the principle that (as Cave put it) 'a true *Specimen* [is] as satisfactory as the whole Parcel'.[2] Cave found a ready audience, both in London and the provinces: Johnson himself later estimated that a monthly issue would sell 10,000 copies (*Life*, III.322). In light of the then population of Great Britain, which grew from around 6.2 million to 7.43 million in the first half of the eighteenth century,[3] that would give it a per issue circulation proportionally not much less than the *Guardian* or *Financial Times* today. In 1736, Johnson advertised his school at Edial in its

23

pages, but even earlier, in 1734, he wrote to Cave – pseudonymously and, as it turned out, unsuccessfully – asking if the magazine might be interested in publishing his work.

It would be easy to portray Cave as an unattractive, small-minded figure. Since most of the *GM* consisted, in effect, of cut-and-pasted work from elsewhere, he faced constant accusations of plagiarism. And he certainly lacked social graces, as several anecdotes attest: Cave once remarked to a writer, 'I hear you have just published a pamphlet, and am told there is a very good paragraph in it, upon the subject of music: did you write that yourself?'[4] The legends around the *GM* could give the impression that Cave worked his writers with the harshness of a stereotypical Victorian factory owner. John Hawkesworth, for instance, contributed poems and translations and worked as a kind of co-editor alongside Cave in the mid to late 1740s; for his labours, he was never paid more than £30 a year – a sum whose smallness would, he said, 'astonish' those who learnt of it.[5]

In his influential if misleading essay on Dr Johnson, Lord Macaulay luxuriated in describing the indigence of the London author:

> To lodge in a garret up four pair of stairs ... to translate ten hours a day for the wages of a ditcher; to be hunted by bailiffs from one haunt of beggary and pestilence to another ... to die in a hospital, and to be buried in a parish vault, was the fate of more than one writer.[6]

That impression is reinforced by Johnson's own grumblings about his life working for the *GM* and on translation projects like Crousaz's *Commentary* (see Chapter 4). In the summer of 1739, he tried to leave London journalism, applying for a teaching job and, when that failed, spending six months in the Midlands not working. He was reported to have said that he would rather 'die upon the road, *than be starved to death in translating for booksellers*; which has been his only subsistence for some time past' (*Life*, I.133).

His early work for the magazine was indeed well beneath his abilities. He had first got to know Cave in 1737 when Johnson proposed to translate Paolo Sarpi's *History of the Council of Trent*. The translation was commissioned but never completed. His first known contribution, however, was 'Ad Urbanum', a piece of flattery saluting Cave's 'learned brow' and advising him to disdain rival publications – the *London Magazine* and *Common Sense* – which accused the *GM* of plagiarism (and of being poor value for money). Johnson's adulation did the trick: he was soon being asked for other small contributions and by around June 1738 had risen to become, in effect, Cave's right-hand man. Before long, he had emerged as, to quote the editors of the

Yale *Works*, 'the de facto editor of the *Gentleman's Magazine* and often its most important contributor' (*Works*, XIX.289).

Later that year, Johnson was again defending the *GM* against plagiarism claims. His riposte was that, after all, the *GM* was the first publication of its kind, so its rivals were the real thieves. 'That these plagiaries should after having thus stolen their whole design from us, charge us with robbery, on any occasion, is a degree of impudence scarcely to be matched, and certainly entitles them to the first rank among false heroes' (*Works*, XX.30–1). What is most startling is the dullness of Johnson's prose. Later, he showed a mastery of satirical writing, an ability to flatten his opponents' arguments without over-statement or mere insults. Here, it doesn't sound like his heart is really in it.

The same goes for much of his other early *GM* work. According to J. D. Fleeman's *Bibliography*, in each year between 1738 and 1743 Johnson made around twenty-five contributions to the magazine. These include poems, book reviews, editorial essays, biographies, advertisements, and letters to the editor (in a sense, letters to himself). But although these were the years in which Johnson's career began to take shape, his daily editorial tasks, and many of his writing assignments, were boringly unglamorous. No wonder he considered fleeing.

Still, to work for the *GM* wasn't necessarily to starve while churning out rubbish. Cave appreciated Johnson's labours enough to pay him reasonably, and at times Johnson was able to write on a congenial subject. A commentary on a recent address by Parliament to the king, for instance, turns into a thoughtful meditation on grief and the dos and don'ts of expressing sympathy with the bereaved ('Pamphilus on Condolence', *Works*, X.3–14).

Moreover, Johnson's flattery of Cave was partly sincere: he found much to admire in the *GM*. Much later, as an established author and scholar about to publish the *Dictionary*, Johnson wrote a biography of Cave which affectionately praised his old boss – his calm determination and perseverance – and, in a tender moment, described how 'one of the last acts of reason which he exerted, was fondly to press the hand which is now writing this little narrative' (*Works*, XIX.300).

Johnson's liking for Cave was partly respect for the older man's skill in finding an audience: the *GM* had become 'one of the most successful and lucrative pamphlets which literary history has upon record' (XIX.298), with a format 'known wherever the English language is spoken' (297). Yet Johnson's 'reverence' went beyond Cave's business acumen. He must also have admired the publication's ambition to be a thorough record of history, to faithfully and impartially set down the events of the time.[7] In a 1751 essay, Johnson suggested that this was the function of 'humble authors':

> If it is necessary for every man to be more acquainted with his contemporaries than with past generations, and to rather know the events which may immediately affect his fortune or quiet, than the revolutions of antient kingdoms, in which he has neither possessions nor expectations; if it be pleasing to hear of the preferment and dismission of statesmen, the birth of heirs, and the marriage of beauties, the humble author of journals and gazettes must be considered as a liberal dispenser of beneficial knowledge.   (*Rambler* 145, *Works*, V.11)

Johnson would sometimes strike a more cynical note. In a 1756 piece for the *Universal Visiter*, 'Reflections on the present state of literature', he commented wearily that no qualification was now necessary to write for the public: 'the inclosures of literature are thrown open to every man whom idleness disposes to loiter, or whom pride inclines to set himself to view' (*Works*, XX.256–7). Yet he recognized that the increase in journalism could also provide harmless entertainment and helpful knowledge.

Through his years of working with Cave, Johnson developed his sense, which informed so much of his later writing, that everyday journalism, however ephemeral, still possessed a certain dignity. In the *Dictionary*, he defined 'Grubstreet' – the once-geographical, later mythical name for the home of small-time journalism – as a word for 'any mean production'. But then, in one of the *Dictionary*'s rare personal flourishes, he half-jokingly quotes an anonymous line of Greek poetry, which translates as 'Hail, Ithaca! after many labours, after bitter suffering, gladly I touch your shore.'[8] Odysseus on Grub Street: there was a hidden grandeur to these apparently 'mean' labours.

Johnson expanded on that point in a 1758 article for the *Universal Chronicle*, 'Of the Duty of a Journalist'. A journalist 'is an historian', and as such must tell the truth – since what a journalist says will sway public opinion (*Works*, XX.406). In particular, journalists should not publish false accounts of robberies and murders: this kind of sensationalism will corrupt readers' morals. 'These scriblers, who give false alarms, ought to be taught, by some public animadversion, that to relate crimes is to teach them, and that as most men are content to follow the herd, and to be like their neighbours, nothing contributes more to the frequency of wickedness, than the representation of it as already frequent' (XX.407). Clarity is essential to writing; so, Johnson adds in a throwaway phrase, is a commitment to 'instruct' the reader, and he promises the readers of the *Universal Chronicle* to 'sell more instruction at a cheaper rate' than other journalists (XX.408). Moral teaching is never far from Johnson's thoughts.

Good journalism can also raise the tone of national conversation. In 1743, writing a preface to a collection of the previous year's *GM* issues, Johnson celebrated the magazine's achievement in recording events and publishing a high quality of poetry (*Works*, XX.107). The following year, he made a more general statement: the rest of the press was lending too much attention to battles between political factions, until 'all subjects of conversation, and all kinds of learning have given way to politicks'. Johnson insisted that 'life requires many other considerations, and that politicks may be said to usurp the mind, when they leave no room for any other subject'. Enter the *GM*, which had 'interspersed political controversies with dissertations on morality, commerce and philosophy' (XX.112).

Not that Johnson thought political discussions unimportant. In his Preface to an index of the first twenty *GM* issues, he claimed that the magazine had 'ascertained the right of the crown and the privileges of the people, so as for ever to prevent their being confounded in the cause either of tyranny or of faction' (*Works*, XX.223–4). One way it had managed this was through the work which took up more of Johnson's labours on the *GM* than any other: the reporting of parliamentary debates.

Such reporting was, strictly speaking, illegal: Cave himself had been jailed and fined in his earlier life for passing the details of parliamentary proceedings to the *Gloucester Journal*, and he would again in 1747 be hauled before the bar in the House of Lords for violating their 'privilege' of secrecy. This was long before the days of the House of Commons press gallery. Yet Cave had his informers in Parliament, who were able to transmit notes on the latest debates. To escape the authorities, Cave then had these written up in a transparently fictionalized form, the 'Debates in the Senate of Lilliput'. At the end of 1740, Johnson took up the task of half-reporting, half-creating these reports. In all, his reports come to almost half a million words, a massive body of work which gave him some moral qualms: later in life, he would speak with unease of the element of untruthfulness, and – perhaps more playfully – wrote much later for another publication, *The Literary Magazine*: 'The speeches inserted in other papers have been long known to be fictitious, and produced sometimes by men who never heard the debate, nor had any authentic information. We have no design to impose thus grosly on our readers' (*Works*, XX.264–5). The Yale edition, it should be said, compares Johnson's accounts as far as possible with eyewitness accounts preserved by a member, and finds the distortion less than one would assume given Johnson's famous remark that he would not 'let the Whig dogs have the best of it'.[9]

If the idea of reporting on Parliament was mischievous, the reality was often formulaic and humdrum. Pitched battles between the shifting Whig factions, and debates 'on the second reading [of] a bill to prevent inconveniencies arising from insurance of ships' or 'a motion in the committee for supplies to grant pay for 16000 Hanevroan [i.e. Hanoverian] troops for four months past' were difficult to enliven. On the other hand, there were some exciting moments – usually reported long after the event in order to reduce the chance of prosecution. The debate in the House of Commons on the motion to remove Robert Walpole, reported in 1743, two years after the event, is genuinely dramatic (*Works*, XII.477–582). After an exposition of all the crimes of which Walpole was accused – his corruption, his hateful excise tax, his weakness in dealing with Spain – the man himself comes forward and makes a pathetic, unctuous defence, referring to his splendid country estate as 'a little house at a small distance from this city' and his dazzling Order of the Garter badge as 'the little ornament upon my shoulder' (XII.580–1). The motion fails, and Johnson recounts the feeble excuses of Tories who voted with the majority. Most of the debates, however, are less thrillingly contentious.

The sea of words in the debates is vast, and there are not exactly gems on every page, but it is possible to sense Johnson learning his craft as a prose stylist. In particular, his knack for an aphorism begins to emerge. In a debate on 'spirituous liquors', for example, he asserts that 'the natural depravity of human nature has always a tendency from less to greater evil' (*Works*, XIII.1398). These journalistic labours may also have given Johnson a useful training: much of his later writing involves the patient weighing-up of opposing views, in a form which mimics parliamentary debate. Still, as with much of Johnson's early work for the *GM*, it is hard to detect his genius.

But in 1742, almost out of the blue, a different Samuel Johnson emerges. In his review of the *Memoirs* of the well-connected and fabulously wealthy Sarah Churchill, we come across the incisive, shrewd, confidently generalizing style which characterizes Johnson's best productions. After pointing out that autobiography is a notoriously untrustworthy genre, he then suddenly reverses course: 'truth, though not always obvious, is generally discoverable, nor is it any where more likely to be found than in private memoirs, which are generally published at a time when any gross falshood may be detected by living witnesses' (*Works*, XX.68).

Next, Johnson applauds Churchill's portrait of King William III as greedy, rude, and untrustworthy. Johnson teases fans of 'the immortal William', who will find this hard to stomach; but 'they whose honesty or sense enables them to consider impartially the events of his reign' will realize that William deserved to be unpopular. He may have 'protected and enriched' his subjects, but as a person he was simply unpleasant. Perceptive readers, Johnson comments,

> will observe that it is not always sufficient to do right, and that it is often necessary to add gracefulness to virtue. They will recollect how vain it is to endeavour to gain men by great qualities, while our cursory behaviour is insolent and offensive, and that those may be disgusted by little things, who can scarcely be pleased with great. (XX.70)

Here is one of Johnson's lifelong convictions: that 'little things' define more of life than we are willing to admit, whether in high politics or everyday occupations. It is 'by studying little things that we attain the great art of having as little misery and as much happiness as possible' (*Life*, I.433).

This review, written with panache and showcasing some of Johnson's deepest principles, stands out from the rest of his early journalism. It is a kind of preview of the project which would, more than any other, define his journalistic work.

The *Rambler*

'My other works are wine and water,' said Johnson, 'but my *Rambler* is pure wine' (*Life*, I.210n1). Many have since agreed that it was his finest work. C. S. Lewis used to read one instalment every evening before going to bed.[10] Yet the series was composed to a similarly tough schedule as his earlier work. It appeared twice a week between March 1750 and March 1752: Johnson could have been forgiven for running out of subjects. Number 134 opens with the author struggling to think of a topic and putting off the moment of decision: 'I rather wished to think, than thought, upon any settled subject; till at last I was awakened from this dream of study by a summons from the press' (*Works*, IV.345). He chooses to write about procrastination.

By this time, Johnson was well past the drudgery of the *GM* years: his commitment to the magazine had begun to gradually wind down in 1743, when he accepted a different kind of work, preparing a catalogue for the sale of a huge book collection, the Harleian Library. By 1750, when the *Rambler* began, he was – thanks to the *Dictionary* commission – on the long slope upwards to fame and success. To publish as 'Mr Rambler', the erudite, pious, severe but self-aware character whose name was on the essays, was itself a mark of distinction, a pseudonym in the tradition of Addison's *Spectator* and Fielding's *Champion*.

Nevertheless, much of the series is about the struggles of minor writers – against poverty, against rival authors, against their own laziness and vanity; and also the struggle of filling a page with something worth printing. From the opening lines of *Rambler* 1 onwards, it is a series which reflects on the process of its own creation:

> The difficulty of the first address on any new occasion, is felt by every man in his transactions with the world, and confessed by the settled and regular forms of salutation which necessity has introduced into all languages. Judgment was wearied with the perplexity of being forced upon choice, where there was no motive to preference; and it was found convenient that some easy method of introduction should be established, which, if it wanted the allurement of novelty, might enjoy the security of prescription.
>
> Perhaps few authors have presented themselves before the public, without wishing that such ceremonial modes of entrance had been anciently established, as might have freed them from those dangers which the desire of pleasing is certain to produce, and precluded the vain expedients of softening censure by apologies, or rousing attention by abruptness. (*Works*, III.3–4)

As that passage reveals, there is also a vein of self-deprecating humour running through the *Rambler* – sometimes on the surface, sometimes so subtle as to be barely discoverable. Johnson is, after all, playing with the reader: by discussing 'the difficulty of the first address', he has already solved it. Readers can feel they are being let in on a trade secret with a nudge and a wink. Throughout the *Rambler*, Johnson plays versions of this game, bringing the audience onto the stage. A series of obviously made-up correspondents write in, often to insult Mr Rambler himself. One young lady, Bellaria, explains that she has been 'forced' by her aunt to study a bunch of *Rambler*s, which she pretends to do while actually reading a love letter from an admirer (*Rambler* 191). In the twenty-third *Rambler*, Johnson cheerfully admits that some critics have 'begun to remark that he was a solemn, serious, dictatorial writer, without sprightliness or gaiety'.

Many readers will sympathize with those critics. At times, the *Rambler* can seem austere and forbidding: a grand marble structure with no obvious entrance point. It is sometimes described as the eighteenth-century equivalent of a newspaper column, but whereas modern columnists feel an obligation to grab the reader's attention, Johnson seems to have deliberately eschewed many of the tricks of the journalist's trade – gossip, reference to current affairs, and so on. In the final instalment, number 208, he openly admitted as much: 'I have seen the meteors of fashion rise and fall, without any attempt to add a moment to their duration. I have never complied with temporary curiosity, nor enabled my readers to discuss the topick of the day' (*Works*, V.316).

There are, in fact, references to topical matters in the *Rambler*; in particular, Johnson devotes two instalments (nos. 170 and 171) to the misery of London's prostitutes. Yet even when he touches on social issues, they are treated less as burning political questions than as tragedies inviting fundamental judgements of right and wrong, and confronting the reader with matters which should outrage their conscience. For the most part, Johnson writes as though for posterity, avoiding contemporary references and instead aiming for timeless truths.

The *Rambler* is not out to charm or entertain its readers so much as to instruct them. It is a sustained study of human nature and human existence, those questions, great or small, which crop up in every life. Is it better to live in the city or the countryside? How can you be sure you're marrying the right person? What is the best remedy for sorrow? Most of us, if called upon to discourse on these subjects, would very soon lapse into cliché. Yet Johnson consistently finds fresh, surprising, and persuasive answers.

He asks, for instance, how worried we should be about hypocrisy. '[F]or many reasons', *Rambler* 14 points out, 'a man writes much better than he lives' (*Works*, III.75). Theorizing about virtue and courage are always easier than putting them into practice. And yet, Johnson argues, theorizing is still worthwhile; even if you don't practise what you preach, at least the preaching can do some good. A sailor, after all, 'may be confident of the advantages of a voyage, or a journey, without having courage or industry to undertake it, and may honestly recommend to others, those attempts which he neglects himself'.

For Johnson – as this passage implies – writing is a highly practical task: it is about helping the reader to be virtuous, even if the author's own life is a mess. He is also, of course, justifying the project of the *Rambler*: Johnson's aim was to give 'ardour to virtue, and confidence to truth' (no. 208; *Works*, V.320), so why let his own faults stand in the way?

He was, for instance, a highly combative conversationalist, ready to use insults and harsh put-downs to win a debate. Yet the *Rambler* essays on the art of conversation recommend a very different approach. As number 188 puts it, people generally avoid 'the scholar whose knowledge allows no man to fancy he instructs him, the critic who suffers no fallacy to pass undetected, and the reasoner who condemns the idle to thought, and the negligent to attention' (*Works*, V.221). Conversationalists who provoke awe or fear are unlikely to receive many dinner invitations; people would rather spend time with the cheerful and good-natured, those who inspire friendliness and fellow feeling.

Moreover, says Johnson, that is only as it should be – since 'it is always necessary to be loved, but not always necessary to be reverenced' (V.224). Though himself a scholar and an awe-inspiring talker, Johnson thought humankind was right to avoid his sort and prefer less distinguished chit-chat.

Johnson returned more than once to this question of what keeps the wheels of social life well oiled. A large part of our lives, *Rambler* 72 notes, 'passes in little incidents, cursory conversation, slight business, and casual amusements'. It is of some importance, then, in what atmosphere we pass these casual hours, and the people who produce the best atmosphere are the good-humoured:

> Good humour may be defined as a habit of being pleased ... It is well known that the most certain way to give any man pleasure, is to persuade him that you receive pleasure from him, to encourage him to freedom and confidence, and to avoid any such appearance of superiority as may overbear and depress him. (*Works*, IV.13–14)

Indeed, says Johnson, the great thing about good humour is precisely that it involves no special skill and so can bring 'friendship to the worthless, and affection to the dull' (IV.16). The *Rambler* is written for the benefit of all humanity, not just the sharp-witted and gifted.

When Johnson refers to writers and scholars in the *Rambler*, it is generally to warn them against envy, vanity, living in their own heads – above all, thinking themselves different from everyone else. The bedrock assumption of these essays is that we are all in the same boat; that, despite all the differences of upbringing, wealth, luck, and talent, 'We all enter the world in equal ignorance, gaze round about us on the same objects, and have our first pains and pleasures, our first hopes and fears, our first aversions and desires from the same causes' (*Rambler* 151, *Works*, V.38–9). Even as we grow older, and as we refine our opinions and tastes, we still understand the world and respond to it with our fickle minds and our mortal bodies.

Because of his belief in the uniformity of the human predicament, Johnson confidently tackles questions which might seem too complex to generalize about. For instance, what is the best way to deal with sorrow (no. 47)? Johnson's starting point, as so often, is our nature as social beings (see Chapter 6). Since we are able to love, we can also be deeply hurt by losing family and friends. Sorrow is, then, 'to a certain point laudable, as the offspring of love' (*Works*, III.255). But only to a certain point: once someone falls into permanent gloom, they will struggle to carry out their 'social duties', to be a good friend or a diligent worker.

Next, the essay surveys the various remedies suggested by other writers. Perhaps we should avoid 'joy' altogether, to avoid distress when it is taken away. No, Johnson responds, sadness will make its way into our life whatever we do, so we might as well try to find some happiness as well. Should the unhappy compel themselves to cheer up, going out to parties and forcing 'the heart . . . into scenes of merriment'? Johnson doubts that this actually works in practice. Should they, instead, put things in perspective by thinking about people who are in an even worse state? This could work, Johnson remarks, but it might also make you permanently miserable (III.257).

At this point, it might be expected that Johnson would invoke Christianity as the solution to sorrow or offer some platitude about time being a great healer. Instead, he makes a simple, practical suggestion – keep busy:

> It is commonly observed that, among soldiers and seamen, though there is much kindness, there is little grief; they see their friend fall without any of that lamentation which is indulged in security and idleness, because they have no leisure to spare from the care of themselves; and whoever shall keep his thoughts equally busy, will find himself equally unaffected with irretrievable losses. . . . Sorrow is a kind of rust of the soul, which every new idea contributes in its passage to scour away. (III.257–8)

Elsewhere, the series can be more waspish. But his admonitions tend to be quietly but forcefully satirical, and often take the form of short stories (see Chapter 3). *Rambler* 146 imagines a writer who believes the public will be fascinated with his latest book, and goes to a coffee-house to eavesdrop on the conversation:

> he enters the places of mingled conversation, sits down to his tea in an obscure corner, and while he appears to examine a file of antiquated journals, catches the conversation of the whole room. He listens, but hears no mention of his book, and therefore supposes that he has disappointed his curiosity by delay, and that as men of learning would naturally begin their conversation with such a wonderful novelty, they had digressed to other subjects before his arrival. (*Works*, V.13–14)

On it goes, excruciatingly, with the writer hurrying through town eavesdropping – the eighteenth-century equivalent of Googling yourself – but hearing nothing about his book. Finally, he decides to start asking strangers if they have come across the book, not revealing that he is the author. Nobody has read it – though somebody has seen it advertised, and one person has heard of the author, who is apparently 'a man condemned by indigence to write too frequently what he does not understand' (V.14–15). Finally, the author reflects that, after all, the greatest writers have always taken a while to establish their reputation. Yet as the *Rambler* comments, even this is a kind of delusion: if fame ever arrives, it slips away, and after death tends to vanish, so that even the successful are familiar only to professional scholars: 'names which hoped to range over kingdoms and continents shrink at last into cloisters or colleges' (16).

Disappointment is a constant theme of the *Rambler*, and yet – here is the central mystery of the series – many readers find it fortifying and uplifting. How can essays so full of dark, unsentimental realism also be so consoling?

Disappointment and Resolution

The twentieth-century novelist, poet, and critic John Wain, who wrote a biography of Johnson, once remarked that he had suffered from reading too much of the author as a young man.

> When I should have been running forward to embrace life, I was digging a fortification against it. With every reason for optimism, I became a stoical pessimist. Samuel Johnson was my favourite author, my moral hero; Boswell and the *Rambler* were constantly open on my table. Johnson reflected my mood exactly, because he put into dignified and resounding prose the sense of stoical resistance against hopeless odds . . . When Johnson wrote the sentences that rang in my head, he was old, racked with diseases, emotionally shattered by the deaths of those he loved . . . Such a man would make himself ridiculous and contemptible by counterfeiting youthful abandon; but it was just as absurd for me, at the age of twenty, to adopt his granite attitudes.[11]

Admittedly, Johnson was only forty-two when he finished the *Rambler*; but it is true that much of his work, including these essays, treats life as a series of misfortunes, and the mind as a factory of comforting illusions waiting to be exploded. As early as *Rambler* 2, Johnson writes that we are always seeking experiences which turn out to be less than we expected. Anticipation beats reality. 'The natural flights of the human mind are not from pleasure to pleasure, but from hope to hope.' This is especially true for authors, who spend hours labouring over productions which are soon forgotten. 'No place affords a more striking conviction of the vanity of human hopes, than a publick library' (no. 106; *Works*, IV.200). Yet the same kind of let-down awaits everyone. *Rambler* 196 records the 'pity and contempt' with which Johnson hears a young man declare his ambitions – to have fun in his early years, to fall in love and get married, to achieve success and fame, and then to retire in comfort, wise, respected, and content.

> With hopes like these, he sallies jocund into life; to little purpose is he told, that the condition of humanity admits no pure and unmingled

happiness; that the exuberant gaiety of youth ends in poverty or disease; that uncommon qualifications and contrarieties of excellence, produce envy equally with applause; that whatever admiration and fondness may promise him, he must marry a wife like the wives of others, with some virtues and some faults, and be as often disgusted with her vices, as delighted by her elegance. (*Works*, V.260)

This passage epitomizes much of the *Rambler*, in its crushing awareness of how we delude ourselves about the future. Life, the *Rambler* often intimates, is a mystery in which even our own motives and desires are hidden from us (see nos. 87, 135), let alone all the other factors which decide our fate.

And yet, that is only one side of the *Rambler*'s advice. Crucially, Johnson applies the same sceptical approach to our fears, as well as our hopes. Optimism may be a delusion, but so is pessimism. Nobody, he writes, has ever 'found the evils of life so formidable in reality, as they were described to him by his own imagination; every species of distress brings with it some peculiar supports, some unforeseen means of resisting, or power of enduring' (*Rambler* 29, *Works*, III.162). A wise person doesn't think too much about the future.

It might seem irresponsible and rash not to consider a worst-case scenario. But, as Johnson argues in *Rambler* 25, rashness is a lesser problem than cowardice. For the rash soon discover their mistake – if they're incapable of succeeding in a project, they'll get a harsh lesson from reality, whereas timidity

> is a disease of the mind more obstinate and fatal; for a man once persuaded, that any impediment is insuperable, has given it, with respect to himself, that strength and weight which it had not before. He can scarcely strive with vigour and perseverance, when he has no hope of gaining the victory; and since he never will try his strength, can never discover the unreasonableness of his fears. (*Works*, III.138)

No on-the-one-hand-on-the-other-hand here; Johnson insists, again and again, that it is better to try the perhaps-impossible than to hang back. If humans are easily ensnared by delusions – as Johnson believes we are – then we shouldn't only be on our guard against false hopes, but also false fears. '[V]isions of calamity' can take possession of the mind, and while these may sometimes be truthful, often they are only the result of our imagination creating 'groundless terrors' for ourselves (*Rambler* 29; *Works*, III.162). Timidity is remarkably good at finding reasons not to do things. Johnson sums it up in a phrase: 'the perspicacity of cowardice' (*Rambler* 134; *Works*, IV.348).

Despite appearances, then, much of the *Rambler* is forcefully life-affirming. 'Yet such is life, that whatever is proposed, it is easier to find reasons for rejecting than embracing' (*Rambler* 39; *Works*, III.212). All the more reason to make the case for risk-taking, ambition, optimism. In *Rambler* 59, Johnson writes of 'that love of life, which is necessary to the vigorous prosecution of any undertaking' (III.315).

Like everything in Johnson's subtle mind, this principle is complicated in practice. Sometimes, he observes, our shyness can save us from saying or doing something stupid:

> I believe few can review the days of their youth, without recollecting temptations, which shame, rather than virtue, enabled them to resist; and opinions which, however erroneous in their principles, and dangerous in their consequences, they have panted to advance at the hazard of contempt and hatred, when they found themselves irresistibly depressed by a languid anxiety, which seized them at the moment of utterance, and still gathered strength from their endeavours to resist it. (*Rambler* 159; *Works*, V.81)

Nevertheless, for the most part, the *Rambler* stresses the dangers of hesitation more than those of over-eagerness. Life is uncertain, yes, but since failure and success are both unpredictable, we may as well 'drive away despair' (*Rambler* 129; *Works*, IV.325) and try to do our best.

Behind this are two of Johnson's central convictions. The first is about friendship and love, both of which involve the risk of being betrayed or disappointed, but which are too valuable to be given up. In this spirit, Johnson writes that it is better to risk being over-trusting than being over-suspicious: 'it is our duty not to suppress tenderness by suspicion', because tenderness among friends is so important (*Rambler* 67, *Works*, IV.55). *Rambler* 188 echoes that sentiment: 'it is always necessary to be loved' (V.224).

The one thing more important than human friendship, in Johnson's scale of values, is one's relationship with God. This is the second point which explains the *Rambler*'s fundamental optimism: a confidence that God is good and will reward every genuine effort to do the right thing. Not everyone can be a genius, adding great scientific advances or artistic achievements to civilization; 'but to add something, however little, every one may hope; and of every honest endeavour it is certain, that, however unsuccessful, it will be at last rewarded' (*Rambler* 129; *Works*, IV.325). On its close observation of everyday life, the *Rambler* builds a foundation to look out on eternity.

A Lifetime in Journalism

Johnson never again attempted a journalistic project as ambitious, in theme and duration, as the *Rambler*. But his later essay series – the twenty-nine pieces he composed for John Hawkesworth's *Adventurer* series (1752–4) and the ninety-one *Idler* essays (1758–60) introduce a lighter touch. In the *Idler*, and here and there in the *Adventurer*, Johnson uses many of the little devices – gossip, political commentary, reference to current trends – which the *Rambler* had consciously avoided. And he is often playful or relaxed where the *Rambler* had been searching and intense.

Adventurer 67, for instance, takes a theme which the *Rambler* had also addressed: that one should try and achieve something, however insignificant that something is, rather than abandoning the effort as pointless. '[W]hoever he be that has but little in his power, should be in haste to do that little, lest he be confounded with him that can do nothing' (*Works*, II.386). But whereas the *Rambler* might have presented this idea at the end of a carefully constructed argument, in the *Adventurer* it appears almost in passing, as Johnson surveys 'the shops of London' and marvels at their variety.

Similarly, *Idler* 59 revisits a point made by *Rambler* 106, that authors are likely to sink into obscurity. The *Rambler* points to 'a publick library' as proof of the 'vanity of human hopes'; the *Idler* observes that 'Of many writers who filled their age with wonder ... the works are now no longer to be seen, or are seen only amidst the lumber of libraries which are seldom visited' (*Works*, II.183). But whereas the *Rambler* ends with two resounding conclusions – that the best way to ensure a posthumous audience is to describe human nature well; and that the most important thing is to please God with one's writing – the *Idler* fizzles out with an observation that Samuel Butler's *Hudibras* went out of fashion when its topical allusions ceased to be understood.

The later essays are also more relaxed, digressive, and – ironically – rambling. *Adventurer* 39 bounces around the subject of sleep, sometimes joking, sometimes arguing, sometimes speculating (perhaps everyone gets the same amount of sleep, so that if you sleep less during the night you are half-asleep for much of the day?), bringing in wherever possible some nugget from Johnson's voluminous reading. Here is a quote from Statius, here is a line from the Italian doctor Ramazzini, here is a story about the polymath Barretier.

Johnson was also readier, in these later essays, to address great moral evils – *Adventurer* 50 is a dire warning against the sin of lying – and urgently topical themes (the *Idler*'s attacks on imperialist exploitation are detailed in Chapter 6). More playful is *Idler* 10, a timeless portrayal of 'political zealots', that is, 'men, who, being numbered, they know not how nor why, in any of the parties that divide a state, resign the use of their own eyes and ears, and resolve to believe nothing that does not favour those whom they profess to follow' (II.33). Johnson sketches caricatures of two kinds of zealot: 'Tom Tempest', a Jacobite full of conspiracy theories ('Of Queen Anne, he ... owns that she meant well, and can tell by whom and why she was poisoned'), and 'Jack Sneaker', a fervent Whig who is 'hourly disturbed by the dread of Popery' (II.34–5). The essay has a general observation at its heart – that political partisanship distorts our ability to distinguish between truth and falsehood – but it ends up as a comic turn.

The *Idler*, unlike Johnson's other essay series, was published as a feature in a newspaper, rather than as a stand-alone essay; and it resembles a newspaper column more than the *Rambler*, partly because of its chattier tone, and partly because of how often Johnson aims to stir up anger at injustice or cruelty. *Idler* 17 attacks the practice of animal experimentation – professors of medicine 'whose favourite amusement is to nail dogs to tables and open them alive' (II.55). In *Idler* 22, Johnson describes passing a debtors' prison – where those who could not repay their creditors could be imprisoned until they could pay up. Since the debtors were stuck in jail, they often struggled to make such repayments and had to stay in prison indefinitely:

> As I was passing lately under one of the gates of this city, I was struck with horror by a rueful cry, which summoned me 'to remember the poor debtors'.
>
> The wisdom and justice of the English laws are, by Englishmen at least, loudly celebrated; but scarcely the most zealous admirers of our institutions can think that law wise, which when men are capable of work, obliges them to beg. (II.69)

In attacking the institution of the debtors' prison, Johnson pointed to its cruelty – creditors were forcing their debtors to 'rot in jail' out of sheer spite – and its practical inefficacy, since the number of debtors had not been reduced. In doing so, he was calling on society to wake up to how it treated the vulnerable: the essay begins with 'the gates of this city', a symbol of London's greatness, and then satirically invokes 'The wisdom and justice of the English laws'. Johnson loved his country and city, but he wanted the patriotic reader to understand that even in London, even in England, terrible inequalities could flourish.

Some of Johnson's polemics are on less sombre themes. *Idler* 36 takes aim at philosophers whose prose is so knotty as to be unintelligible; *Idler* 40 mocks the advertisements in newspapers, with their solemn announcements about, say, 'Duvets ... [whose] many excellencies cannot be here set forth' (II.125).

Reviews and Occasional Writings

The range of Johnson's essay topics – from morality to literature to politics to duvets – still only represents a portion of his interests. Throughout his life, he produced book reviews, prefaces, public statements, and other examples of minor writing. The scope of these occasional compositions is impressive. In 1756–7, when Johnson was involved with the *Literary Magazine*, he wrote forty-four articles, mostly reviews, on subjects including beekeeping, the natural history of Aleppo, a complex forgery case, bleaching, and travel literature. One little piece, introducing an extract from a book about electricity, begins arrestingly:

> Electricity is the great discovery of the present age, and the great object of philosophical curiosity. It is perhaps designed by providence for the excitement of human industry, that the qualities of bodies should be discovered gradually from time to time.   (*Works*, XX.352–3)

A familiar Johnsonian theme surfaces: the worthiness of 'human industry', which is ordained by 'providence'. But there is another sublime mystery at hand:

> How many wonders may yet lie hid in every particle of matter no man can determine. The power of Electricity is sufficient to shew us that nature is far from being exhausted, and that we have yet much to do before we shall be fully acquainted with the properties of these things which are always in our hands and before our eyes.   (*Works*, XX.353)

Quantum physics – the discovery of yet more properties hidden in the material world – would have thrilled him.

Johnson's enjoyment of scientific experimentation is about more than just curiosity; he is also concerned with the usefulness of technological advances. Reviewing a book by Stephen Hales, who had devised a new means of purifying seawater, Johnson opens admiringly: 'This is another of the labours of a life spent in the service of mankind' (*Works*, XX.338). The detailed review which follows shows Johnson's keen interest in the latest research.

Ever the pragmatist, Johnson as reviewer asks whether the book before him will help the reader. Writing on a new history of the Norman Conquest, Johnson comments tersely: 'This pamphlet is published to prove what nobody will deny, that we shall be less happy if we were conquered by the French' (*Works*, XX.348). Since at that time, in 1756, the army and navy were at full strength and nationalist fervour had reached a high pitch, the book's agenda seemed pointless. Yet, Johnson adds in a gesture of Christian charity, 'The intention of the author is undoubtedly good.' Likewise, Johnson reviews a turgid pamphlet about the national debt by saying it 'seems to be written with a very honest intention by a man better acquainted with arithmetic than with style' (XX.348).

Johnson was capable of writing a harsh review. 'The diversion of baiting an author has the sanction of all ages and nations', he writes in *Rambler* 176, because 'for the most part he comes voluntarily to the stake' (*Works*, V.165). Yet with the exception of Soame Jenyns (see Chapter 6), whose callousness towards the poor shocked him, Johnson prefers to let authors off lightly, often by praising their good intentions. Reviewing Jonas Hanway's essay against tea-drinking, Johnson remarks that it is marred by grammatical mistakes. But 'with us to mean well is a degree of merit which over-balances much greater errors than impurity of stile' – and clearly Hanway means well (*Works*, XX.359). Johnson doesn't think much of Hanway's argument – but he seems a decent man, whose 'failings may well be pardoned for his virtues'.

Only when Hanway fired back, taking issue with these words and pompously insisting on his status as a board member at a well-known children's home, did Johnson lose patience. After all, Johnson said, he had hardly been disrespectful. He had credited Hanway with

> the merit of 'meaning well', and the journalist was declared to be a man 'whose failings might well be pardoned for his virtues'. This is the highest praise which human gratitude can confer upon human merit, praise that would have more than satisfied Titus or Augustus, but which I must own to be inadequate and penurious when offered to the member of an important corporation. (*Works*, XX.373)

Johnson does not, however, end on a sarcastic note: despite Hanway's 'tumultuous resentment', he concludes, 'I still esteem him as one that has the "merit of meaning well", and still believe him to be "a man whose failings may be justly pardoned for his virtues"' (*Works*, XX.376). Here is a final attempt at showing mercy in the midst of controversy.

As the Yale editors observe, many of Johnson's writings were produced 'for others or as parts of the planning or aspects of the reception of others' works'

(*Works*, XX.x). He penned appeals for donations, prefaces to acquaintances' works, book dedications, election material for his friend Henry Thrale. But even when he was writing as a favour or a social duty, his fascination with human nature means he is always seeking to pass on some essential wisdom. One of Johnson's last works was commissioned by his friend Charles Burney: a dedication to the king to stand at the opening of Burney's account of a 1784 music festival, the Handel Commemoration. Many writers composed the dedications to their own works, but others regarded them as belonging to a special genre – like an epitaph – for which one should turn to a trusted professional; and Johnson was the professional writer par excellence. For Burney, as for any other client, Johnson could have dashed off a few sycophantic paragraphs; instead, he drills down to an anthropological observation. Explorers, he notes, always find that remote civilizations have musical traditions. This suggests that, as soon as human societies have any leisure from the struggle for survival, they turn towards music-making. 'The mind set free from the restless tyranny of painful want, employs its first leisure upon some savage melody' (*Works*, XX.543).

In 1748, the publisher Robert Dodsley brought out *The Preceptor*, an all-purpose textbook aiming to lay out the fundamental principles of everything from arithmetic to history to 'human life and manners'. Johnson's Preface to the work breathes a delight in learning and intellectual discovery. He recommends, for instance, that geography should be taught with the help of anecdotes: 'in explaining the state of the polar regions, it might be fit to read the narrative of the Englishmen that wintered in Greenland, which will make young minds sufficiently curious after the cause of such a length of night, and intenseness of cold' (*Works*, XX.179–80). The main use of natural history is 'To excite a curiosity after the works of God' (*Works*, XX.186). Implicitly and explicitly, Johnson returns to one of his guiding literary principles: that the mind, especially when tired, is liable to wander off into pointless or dangerous thoughts, and so teaching should be entertaining but also informative: 'it seems necessary to scatter in its way such allurements as may withhold it from an useless and unbounded dissipation' (*Works*, XX.172). Perhaps, in Dodsley's project for educating the young through allurement as well as instruction, Johnson found an echo of his own calling.

Figure 3.1 Johnson in his late thirties, from the mezzotint by George Zobel. © National Portrait Gallery, London.

Chapter 3

Poet and Storyteller

> To circumscribe poetry by a definition will only shew the narrowness of the definer.
>
> ('Life of Pope', *Lives*, IV.80)

More than any other aspect of his literary career, Johnson's composition of poetry is intertwined with his private life. He wrote poetry from his youth until his final days. The story that he wrote 'the epitaph upon the duck he killed by treading on it at five years old' (*Miscellanies*, I.153) is less than half-true: his father was evidently the author of that poem (*Life*, 1.40). Nevertheless, by fifteen Johnson was writing accomplished verse and continued to do so until he wrote his last poem on 5 December 1784, eight days before his death. As David Venturo points out in the only full-length study of all the poetry, *Johnson the Poet* (1999), only a small fraction of Johnson's verse output was part of his paid professional life as an author, which was conducted mainly in prose. The 'professional pieces' include his most important poetry – *London* (1738), *The Vanity of Human Wishes* (1749), and his verse drama *Irene* (1749) – but most of his other verse tells us more about his personal thoughts and feelings than his professional publications. Admittedly, some of Johnson's non-professional poetry is merely versification – the equivalent of an artist's doodling – but other exercises, many of them in Latin, express his aspirational life as a classical scholar; still others are part of his devotional life. On the proof sheets of the 'Life of Pope', Johnson had written the epigraph to this chapter in a more aggressive way: 'To circumscribe poetry by a definition is the pedantry of a narrow mind' (*Lives*, IV.221). As Roger Lonsdale points out (*Lives*, IV.348), Johnson was still at this late date reacting to Joseph Warton's *Essay on the Writings and Genius of Pope* (1756), which claimed Pope was not a 'true poet' but merely a 'man of wit'. Warton's claim implied in Johnson's view too strict a definition of poetry. At all times, Johnson was reluctant to define poetry, and when he did, he defined it either in very broad or in largely formal terms. When Boswell asked, 'Then, Sir, what is poetry', Johnson replied that 'it is much easier to say what it is not. We all *know* what light is; but it is not easy to *tell* what it is' (*Life*, III.38). In his *Dictionary* definition of 'poetry', Johnson was content to call it 'Metrical composition; the art or practice of writing poems'. The second clause is very unsatisfactory as a definition for obvious reasons, but the first provides a clue to approaching a great deal of Johnson's own verse. He knew that language could be arranged metrically without being poetry. He was sensitive of course to diction, sense, learning, and above all meaning, and he agreed with Aristotle that poetry should imitate life; but most basic of all for Johnson was poetry's appeal to the ear.

This is surprising for some students of Johnson because he was notoriously hard of hearing – and supposedly deaf to the charms of music, though Morris R. Brownell has persuasively rebutted this latter belief.[1] In any event, Johnson could hear poetry with an inward sense more easily than he could hear music, and a great deal of his poetry consists of exercises for the ear. To give a famous example of a trivial poem, Johnson composed a parody of Bishop Percy's ballad 'The Hermit of Warkworth'. Boswell recited the lines to Johnson, telling him he had heard Garrick repeat them in that form. Johnson responded, 'Then he has no ear': Garrick's version was metrically deficient. Johnson then gave Boswell the lines in the following form:

> I put my hat upon my head
>   And walk'd into the Strand
> And there I met another man
>   Whose hat was in his hand.
>
> (*LAEP*, 438)

In the corrupt form, which Boswell said he had from Garrick, the last line is 'With his hat in his hand' (*Boswell Papers*, IX.265).

Johnson composed many other such trivial poems, several of them parodies, and the majority of them extempore, including a couple of Thomas Warton. One of them, written in 1777 in response to Warton's *Poems, A New Edition* (1777), goes:

> Wheresoe'er I turn my view,
> All is strange, yet nothing new:
> Endless Labour all along,
> Endless Labour to be wrong;
> Phrase that Time has flung away;
> Uncouth Words in disarray,
> Trick'd in antique ruff and bonnet,
> Ode, and elegy, and sonnet.
>
> (*LAEP*, 514)

The joke only works because Johnson has captured the rhythm of Warton's poetry, making it more routine, and applied ludicrous words. It takes a good ear to do this.

If these parodies – the lowest class of Johnson's poetry, comprising as much as a quarter of his extant verse – are trivial, they are nonetheless related in spirit to his more important works. In the poems he wrote as exercises to soothe or distract himself from physical or spiritual pain, he often called upon the same sense of rhythm and the same instinct for appropriate diction that inform his light verse. Johnson composed many of his consolatory poems in Latin, which gave him the added distraction of working in a learned language. One of the most notable of these is his 'Prayer on Losing the Power of Speech', written on the night of 16 June 1783 after suffering a stroke. As he wrote to Hester Thrale: 'This prayer, that I might try the integrity of my faculties I made in Latin verse. The lines were not very good, but I knew them not to be very good, I made them easily, and concluded myself to be unimpaired in my faculties' (*Letters*, IV.151).

Related to the parodies and tests of competency, but more impressive and significant, are the approximately 100 translations Johnson made in Latin from the *Greek Anthology* in the winter of 1784. As he told Thrale, 'When I lay sleepless, I used to drive the night along, by turning Greek Epigrams into Latin' (*Letters*, IV.318). Although this work is a learned pastime, it is also impressive and scholarly.

Beyond a pastime are the many prayers that Johnson composed in verse. Quite a number of these are Latin imitations or loose translations of collects in the Book of Common Prayer (see *LAEP*, 601–9). They are expressions of Johnson's late life religious views and very serious, but his effort in making them is largely one of versification rather than invention. Johnson's last poem is a paraphrase in verse of the collect of the Communion Service in the Book of Common Prayer. It reads in full:

> Summe Deus, cui caeca patent penetralia cordis;
>   Quem nulla anxietas, nulla cupido fugit;
> Quem nil vafrities peccantum subdola celat;
>   Omnia qui spectans, omnia ubique regis;
> Mentibus afflatu terrenas ejice sordes
>   Divino, sanctus regnet ut intus amor:
> Eloquiumque potens linguis torpentibus affer,
>   Ut tibi laus omni semper ab ore sonet:
> Sanguine quo gentes, quo secula cuncta piavit,
>   Haec nobis Christus promeruisse velit!

> Almighty God, to whom the hidden recesses of the heart lie open, whom no anxiety, no desire escapes, from whom the crafty guile of sinners keeps nothing concealed, who, seeing all things, rule all things everywhere: by your divine inspiration rid our minds of earthly

impurities, so that holy love may reign within us. Bring powerful eloquence to sluggish tongues, so that your praise may always resound from every mouth. Through the blood by which he has cleansed the nations and the ages, may Christ be willing to earn these things for us. (*LAEP*, 701)

The Young Author

> So the young author panting for a name,
> And fir'd with pleasing hope of endless fame,
> Intrusts his happiness to human kind,
> More false, more cruel than the seas and wind.
>
> ('The Young Author', lines 11–14)

Most of Johnson's extempore poems – parodies, pastimes, and consolations – date from his late life. Early in his life, he wrote some courtly love poems and many translations, mainly of the greatest Roman writers, and above all Horace, the author he returned to most often throughout his life. Most of these early poems were unpublished in his lifetime, and the majority were exercises that scarcely rise above the baseline of poetry as versification. One curious oddity among the juvenilia is Johnson's translation of Joseph Addison's Latin poem on the battle of the pygmies and the cranes. Addison's poem is a kind of mock epic based on a pseudo-Homeric parody of the *Iliad*: in high Virgilian language, Addison relates a war between ludicrously small opponents. Johnson's translation is his only poem in the epic genre and shows the sort of heights, and depths, to which his poetry would never go again. It opens:

> Feather'd Battalions, Squadrons on the wing
> And the sad fate of Pygmie Realms I sing;
> Direct, O Goddess, my advent'rous song,
> In warring Colours shew the warring throng;
>
> (*LAEP*, 71)

Addison, so important to Johnson as a forerunner, would later write poetry such as *The Campaign* that sincerely depicts the glory of battle, but Johnson would never go there. His métier remained satire, except when his subject was religion, as it is in his Latin translation of Alexander Pope's *Messiah*.

Another early poem that deserves attention is 'The Young Author'. Some critics have thought the poem is a response to Johnson's departure from Oxford without a degree in 1729. This may or may not be so, but 'The

Young Author' is important in Johnson's body of poetry because it reads as a sketch for the section on the student in *The Vanity of Human Wishes*. Johnson compares the 'young author' to a 'peasant' who leaves his native home to venture abroad by ship. Inevitably, storms arise: 'Sick'ning with fear he longs to view the shore, / And vows to trust the faithless deep no more' (lines 9–10). The young author ventures out on the sea of publication and inevitably:

> The pamphlet spreads, incessant hisses rise,
> To some retreat the baffled writer flies,
> Where no sour criticks damn, nor sneers molest,
> Safe from the keen lampoon and stinging jest;
> There begs of heav'n a less distinguish'd lot;
> Glad to be hid, and proud to be forgot.
>
> (lines 25–30)

Johnson would later rehearse this theme not only in *The Vanity of Human Wishes* but in numerous *Rambler*s and *Idler*s. In every case, even writers who get further along than the 'young author' eventually sink painfully into obscurity. As Johnson put it in *Idler* 59, 'Of many writers who filled their age with wonder, and whose names we find celebrated in the books of their contemporaries, the works are now no longer to be seen, or are seen only amidst the lumber of libraries which are seldom visited, where they lie only to shew the deceitfulness of hope, and the uncertainty of honour' (*Works*, II.183). Johnson wrote those words in June 1759, ten years after publishing *The Vanity of Human Wishes*. By then, he had been honing the theme for thirty years.

He was still a young author full of hope when he published his first important poem, *London*, in 1738. He had been in London for only a year, but he had made important connections. Most important of all in his early career was Edward Cave, the proprietor of the *Gentleman's Magazine*. Johnson had initially approached him with an offer to improve the poetry section of the magazine, and accordingly he wrote Latin and Greek poems addressed to both Cave and two of the writers in his circle, Elizabeth Carter and Richard Savage. Johnson submitted *London* to Cave in March 1738. Cave was favourably impressed and showed it to Robert Dodsley, a more important publisher, who could distribute the poem more widely than Cave. When the poem was published on 13 May 1738, Dodsley was the publisher (or, more properly, bookseller) and Cave was the printer. Dodsley also happened to be the principal publisher of Alexander Pope at this time, and he released Pope's latest imitation of Horace, *One Thousand Seven Hundred and Thirty Eight*.

A Dialogue Something Like Horace, at exactly the same time. The pairing was prescient because Johnson would become Pope's successor as the principal writer in Dodsley's stable, but the immediate intention and effect was to elevate Johnson into the world of the age's most famous poet. Pope commented generously on the anonymously published *London* and declared that its author would 'soon be *déterré*' – that is, discovered (*Life*, I.128–9). It was indeed through *London* that Johnson became a name to reckon with; in fact, he was known primarily as 'the author of *London*' for the next ten years.

London

> When a man is tired of London, he is tired of life.
> (*Life*, III.178)

London is an imitation of a satire by the first-century Roman author Juvenal, whose fifteen extant verse satires – though they vary in tone and topic – are known for their sharp vituperation and shocking detail. The third satire, which Johnson chose to imitate, is largely political, focusing on corruption, decay, and degradation in the city of Rome. One of Johnson's *Dictionary* definitions of 'imitation' was '3. A method of translating looser than paraphrase, in which modern examples and illustrations are used for ancient, or domestick for foreign.' He replaced Juvenal's Rome with London and made other appropriate substitutions. John Oldham (1653–83) had performed the same procedure, and before him Nicolas Boileau-Despréaux (1636–1711) had changed Juvenal's Rome into Paris in his first satire. As in most of his poetry, but perhaps to an unusual extent, Johnson was following in the footsteps of others. In fact, the pleasure in reading the poem for many of his contemporaries must have been to see how Johnson was transforming Juvenal and, if the readers were sharp enough, differing in his methods from Oldham and Boileau.

Indeed, Johnson had the publisher print the relevant passages from Juvenal alongside his own imitation. (It was a given of imitation that not every part of the poem imitated had to be used.) The presence of the Latin makes Johnson's project partly scholarly commentary, connecting it with his original dream of joining the great humanist scholar-poets; but *London* also has a literary and polemical character of its own. As literature, Johnson's transformation elevates Juvenal by infusing the poem with a characteristically Johnsonian feature: abstractions which almost take on the quality of personifications. Johnson also elevates Juvenal by changing the principal speaker from

Umbricius, a venal soothsayer, to Thales, one of the seven wise men of Greece. The high-toned language of Thales in his opening speech sets the temper of Johnson's imitation:

> Since worth, he cries, in these degen'rate days,
> Wants ev'n the cheap reward of empty praise;
> In those curst walls, devote to vice and gain,
> Since unrewarded science toils in vain;
> Since hope but sooths to double my distress,
> And ev'ry moment leaves my little less;
> While yet my steady steps no staff sustains,
> And life still vig'rous revels in my veins;
> Grant me, kind heaven, to find some happier place,
> Where honesty and sense are no disgrace;
> Some pleasing bank where verdant osiers play,
> Some peaceful vale with nature's paintings gay;
> Where once the harrass'd Briton found repose,
> And safe in poverty defy'd his foes;
> Some secret cell, ye pow'rs, indulgent give.
>
> (lines 35–49)

'Worth', 'science', 'hope' all approach personification because they 'want', 'toil', or 'soothe', like human beings. There is no equivalent for such language in Juvenal. 'Worth' significantly reappears in the most famous line of the poem, printed entirely in capital letters: 'SLOW RISES WORTH, BY POVERTY DEPREST' (177). The line has autobiographical overtones: Johnson could see himself as an embodiment of Worth at this stage of his career. His insertion of himself into the translation could even be viewed as metatextual or postmodern. However, the trope of light personification that became part of Johnson's brand – his trademark language – is more important than the autobiographical suggestion.

The pastoral longings in this passage are also notable, especially for a writer who famously despised pastoral poetry. As in much of the poem, Johnson's intent here was political. In some lines, admittedly, Johnson makes fun of these pastoral longings, as when he asks rhetorically and ironically, 'For who would leave, unbrib'd, Hibernia's land,/ Or change the Rocks of Scotland for the Strand?' (lines 9–10). Mainly, however, the wish to go into the country is a staple of Tory rhetoric, dating back to the Civil War when Royalist poets such as George Herrick used country life as a metaphor for pre-war Jacobean peace. The urban villains in *London* are not the Puritans but Robert Walpole and the Whigs, who were largely in power from 1721 to 1741 with the support of the Hanoverian kings, George I and II. Johnson alludes to several much-criticized aspects of Whiggish government – the pension, the excise tax, the Ways and Means allocation committee in Parliament, the Licensing Act, and the government publicity organ, the *Gazette* – as he rehearses the fantasy of removal to the country.

His indignation was certainly genuine: at the time, Johnson was about to publish two fiercely anti-government pamphlets, and he later recalled walking the streets at night and proclaiming patriot (i.e. anti-government) slogans with Richard Savage, whose life he would write in 1744. Savage was long thought to be the Thales of *London*. That is chronologically unlikely, but the association is right. Even so, their positions were wrapped up in their identities as authors: *London* is partly a pledge of loyalty to the publishers and writers of London whom Johnson was joining. He and Savage were not only political bedfellows; they were members of the same fraternity of authors. It is significant that Savage subscribed for ten copies of Husband's *Miscellany* featuring Johnson's first poem (his translation of Pope's *Messiah*), and that Johnson wrote a poem to Savage for publication in the *Gentleman's Magazine*. At the end of *London*, Johnson shows how much his work was about the Author in London, to whose class he belonged:

> Farewell! – When youth, and health, and fortune spent,
> Thou fly'st for refuge to the wilds of Kent;
> And tir'd like me with follies and with crimes,
> In angry numbers warn'st succeeding times;
> Then shall thy friend, nor thou refuse his aid,
> Still foe to vice, forsake his Cambrian shade;
> In virtue's cause once more exert his rage,
> Thy satire point, and animate thy page.
>
> (lines 256–63)

Thales has become a writer himself, and a comrade of *London*'s author. In the imagined future, they will both be in the country exerting their talent on behalf of virtue, employing the *saeva indignatio* (fierce indignation) of Swift and other publishing satirists.

Vanity of Human Wishes

Satire was again Johnson's chosen mode in his second imitation of Juvenal, his most important poem. *The Vanity of Human Wishes* is the quintessentially Johnsonian work, being the most eloquent and most compressed exposition of the central theme in his literary works. He expressed his familiarity (bordering on contempt) for the theme in *Rambler* 66: 'The folly of human wishes and persuits has always been a standing subject of mirth and declamation, and has been ridiculed and lamented from age to age; till perhaps the fruitless repetition of complaints and censures may be justly numbered among the subjects of complaint and censure' (*Works*, III.349). Even contemptuous familiarity, however, could not remove the topic from Johnson's view; he kept it in mind and in his poetry forever. The theme was, as it were, his own death's head, a memento mori, kept in view to make himself and others better people.

Johnson finished his great poem in November 1748, and it was published in January of the next year. He provided this account of its composition as part of a statement about his general method of poetic composition:

> When composing [verses], I have generally had them in my mind, perhaps fifty at a time, walking up and down in my room; and then I have written them down, and often, from laziness, have written only half lines. I have written a hundred lines in a day. I remember I wrote a hundred lines of 'The Vanity of Human Wishes' in a day. (*Life*, II.15)

This suggests that Johnson's way of making poetry was often, as we said earlier, a mode of versification. Such composition is obvious with his trivial parodies and other extempore poems, but it is surprising in the case of a long and important poem like the *Vanity*. Johnson, however, was so familiar with the theme and with his Juvenalian model that the task required little forethought. His task was to produce, in the words of Pope's 'Essay on Criticism', 'What oft was *Thought* but ne'er so well *Exprest*'.

The tenth satire is Juvenal's grandest and most philosophical poem. Johnson elevated it further, as he had elevated his imitation of the third satire, by the use of abstraction and personification. In his 'Life of Dryden' thirty years later, Johnson would say, 'The peculiarity of Juvenal is a mixture of gaiety and stateliness, of pointed sentences, and declamatory grandeur' (*Lives*, II.143). His imitation ratchets up both the grandeur and pointedness of Juvenal, who at times can seem needlessly crude. Johnson chose this time not to print the Latin passages that he imitated but merely to refer at the foot of the page to the relevant lines of Juvenal by number. The poem stands on its own, therefore, somewhat more independently than *London*. In its Johnsonian form, Juvenal's tenth satire becomes a prolonged meditation on the biblical verse 'Vanity of vanities, saith the Preacher, vanity of vanities; all is vanity' (Ecclesiastes 1:2).

Whereas Juvenal's opening is stately and general, in his first lines Johnson is already moving towards the mode of allegory. The scene is like something out of Dante or, to bring it closer to Johnson's English milieu, Bunyan:

> Then say how hope and fear, desire and hate,
> O'erspread with snares the clouded maze of fate,
> Where wav'ring man, betray'd by vent'rous pride,
> To tread the dreary paths without a guide;
> As treach'rous phantoms in the mist delude,
> Shuns fancied ills, or chases airy good.
>
> (lines 10–15)

In the poem's first edition, 'hope' and 'fear' were capitalized, to further the effect of personification. With or without capitals, however, it is easy to visualize the crepuscular scene in which man is lost. His passions are projected so that they beset him from without: they are described as operating against a mazy, hazy backdrop.

As the poem moves on, the abstract man of the opening is replaced by a series of more specific characters, some merely types and others historical personages: 'the needy traveler' (37), 'the sinking statesman' (79), Cardinal Wolsey (99), Charles XII (192), 'Great Xerxes' (227), Charles Albert of Bavaria (241), a man who prays for long life (255–6), and a beauty like Catherine Sedley or Anne Vane (321–2). Many other figures, such as Swift and Marlborough, make cameo appearances, and all show the vanity of typical human wishes: power, money, beauty, long life, prestige, and fame. The most deeply felt of all the figures in the poem, however, is the student, who makes his appearance on line 135. Hester Thrale Piozzi reported that Johnson 'burst into a passion of tears' when reading this passage aloud later in life (*Miscellanies*, I.180):

> When first the college rolls receive his name,
> The young enthusiast quits his ease for fame;
> Through all his veins the fever of renown
> Burns from the strong contagion of the gown;
> O'er Bodley's dome his future labours spread,
> And Bacon's mansion trembles o'er his head.
> Are these thy views? proceed, illustrious youth,
> And virtue guard thee to the throne of Truth!
> Yet should thy soul indulge the gen'rous heat,
> Till captive Science yields her last retreat;
> Should Reason guide thee with her brightest ray,
> And pour on misty Doubt resistless day;

> Should no false Kindness lure to loose delight,
> Nor Praise relax, nor Difficulty fright;
> Should tempting Novelty thy cell refrain,
> And Sloth effuse her opiate fumes in vain;
> Should Beauty blunt on fops her fatal dart,
> Nor claim the triumph of a letter'd heart;
> Should no Disease thy torpid veins invade,
> Nor Melancholy's phantoms haunt thy shade;
> Yet hope not life from grief or danger free,
> Nor think the doom of man revers'd for thee.
>
> (lines 135–56)

One sign of the importance of this passage to Johnson personally is that it represents the most radical departure from Juvenal's poem. In Juvenal, there is a young scholar who wishes for the eloquence of Demosthenes and Cicero, but Juvenal shows that those famous orators met miserable fates; he does not portray the scholar, whereas Johnson gives him lavish treatment. As Johnson tells it, even if the student avoids all the ills of a scholarly life – 'loose delight', 'tempting novelty', 'Sloth', romance, 'Disease', and 'Melancholy' – he cannot escape 'the doom of man'. In the end he is commanded to

> Deign on the passing world to turn thine eyes,
> And pause awhile from letters, to be wise;
> There mark what ills the scholar's life assail,
> Toil, envy, want, the patron, and the jail.
>
> (lines 157–60)

Johnson inserted 'patron' for 'garret' when he revised the poem in 1755, presumably as a response to Lord Chesterfield's failure to support his work on the *Dictionary*. In either version, however, the ironic antithesis between 'letters' (i.e. learning) and wisdom distils the pathos of the scholar's life and completes in allegorical fashion the picture Johnson began to sketch in 'The Young Author'.

Interpretation of the ending of *The Vanity of Human Wishes* has been much contested. Juvenal's conclusion emphasizes the Stoical values of resignation and emotional control and advises the reader to make wishes that do not lead to suffering. Johnson clearly departs from his model, recommending instead the Christian virtues of love, faith, hope, and patience.

> Pour forth thy fervours for a healthful mind,
> Obedient passions, and a will resign'd;
> For love, which scarce collective man can fill;
> For patience sov'reign o'er transmuted Ill;

> For faith, that panting for a happier seat,
> Counts death kind Nature's signal of retreat:
> These goods for man the laws of heav'n ordain,
> These goods he grants, who grants the pow'r to gain;
> With these celestial wisdom calms the mind,
> And makes the happiness she does not find.
>
> (lines 359–68)

For some readers, this ending shows the depth of Johnson's Christianity and his rejection of the satirical, if not nihilistic, worldview that permeates the rest of Johnson's poem and all of Juvenal's. For others, the ending is a concession to the expectations of an audience more inclined to approve Christian optimism than a tragic view of what later pessimists would call the 'human predicament'. There are good arguments on either side, but it is important to remember that the *Vanity* is one of Johnson's relatively few public poems. In private, Johnson was more likely to emphasize doubt and bewilderment, as in 'Know thyself', the poem he addressed to Joseph Scaliger in 1773, after completing his revision of the *Dictionary*. There he describes his mind or his soul shuddering as it contemplates a vast silent night:

> – ubi vanae species, umbraeque fugaces,
> Et rerum volitant rarae per inane figurae
>
> (lines 50–1)
>
> where empty visions, fleeting shadows, and insubstantial shapes of things flit through the void.
>
> (*LAEP*, 455–7)

In this poem, religion does not come to the rescue, and for solace Johnson ends up with a seeming resolve to return to lexicographical drudgery. This does not mean that Johnson was not deeply religious. In fact, much of his late poetry testifies to his religious sincerity, but his greatest poem, *The Vanity of Human Wishes*, is fundamentally satirical and ironic despite the optimistic ending, just as *King Lear* is fundamentally tragic despite the romantic ending supplied by Nahum Tate that eighteenth-century viewers and readers – including Johnson – preferred to witness.

'On the Death of Dr. Robert Levet'

> His virtues walk'd their narrow round.
> ('On the Death of Dr. Robert Levet', line 25)

One more poem demands attention in any introduction to Johnson's poetry. In 1782, Johnson's old housemate Robert Levet died suddenly, and Johnson soon responded with an elegy. He chose the tetrameter quatrain for his metre, rather than the grander heroic couplet (his usual form), and praised Levet, an unlicensed doctor for the poor, as the humble son who makes good use of his small patrimony in the biblical parable of the talents. This story from Matthew 25:14–30 clearly played on Johnson's mind throughout his life. He saw himself as gifted with much ability and therefore required to show that he had done much with his life. His prayer on beginning the second volume of his *Dictionary* (3 April 1753) is representative: 'O God who hast hitherto supported me enable me to proceed in this labour & in the Whole task of my present state that when I shall render up at the last day an account of the talent committed to me I may receive pardon for the sake of Jesus Christ. Amen' (*Works*, I.50). In Johnson's elegy, Levet is relieved of such worries because he has used his benefaction well.

The poem is set against the same depressing landscape described in *The Vanity*:

> Condemn'd to Hope's delusive mine,
>   As on we toil from day to day,
> By sudden blast, or slow decline,
>   Our social comforts drop away.
>
>   (lines 1–4)

In this world, however, Levet finds the sure way to salvation:

> His virtues walk'd their narrow round,
>   Nor made a pause nor left a void;
> And sure th' Eternal Master found
>   His single talent well employ'd.
>
>   (lines 25–8)

Various critics have seen the poem as an imitation of an Anglican hymn, and clearly it asserts the low church values of simplicity, faith, and good works. Comparison to Thomas Gray's justly famous *Elegy Written in a Country Churchyard* has been inevitable, but, though both poems uphold the value of a simple life well led, Johnson's poem, to a much greater extent than Gray's, embodies the simplicity it asserts. Johnson would take up the same theme in his Latin versification of the collect just quoted (p. 45): 'Summe Deus, cui caeca patent penetralia cordis' ('Almighty God, to whom the secret recesses of the heart lie open'). In his final poems, Johnson seems genuinely to achieve the religious resolution that was arguably a gratuitous addendum to his greatest poem.

Fiction

In his assessment of the different sorts of essays he wrote in the *Rambler*, Johnson rated his 'excursions of fancy' (i.e. the 'oriental tales') lowest in importance. At the other end of the scale were 'the essays professedly serious' and in between he put critical essays and 'pictures of life' (*Works*, V.319–20). Such distinctions are attractive, or as Johnson might put it, 'specious', but neither his essays nor his other writings are so easily categorized. The difficulty of categorization is especially acute when it comes to Johnson's fictions. Few can be described as 'excursions of fancy' because almost all are packed with moral lessons. In fact, most of Johnson's fictions dramatize the essential theme of his serious writings, summed up most succinctly in the *Vanity of Human Wishes*. 'The Fountains', for example, is a kind of fairy tale that Johnson wrote for Anna Williams's *Miscellany*, a production he edited and partly wrote for the benefit of his blind housemate. In this work, Floretta is given numerous wishes by a fairy. She chooses many of the wishes shown to be empty in the *Vanity of Human Wishes*: wealth, beauty, intellectual power, and long life. In the end all is vanity, and Floretta resigns herself to following 'the course of Nature' (*Works*, XVI.249), in effect viewing death as 'kind Nature's signal of retreat' (*Vanity of Human Wishes*, line 364).

'The Fountains', as Gwin Kolb observes in his introduction to the Yale edition, follows the pattern of a story attributed to the fifth-century BCE sophist Prodicus of Ceos, 'The Choice of Hercules'. The ancient hero must choose between pleasure and virtue, and so must Johnson's fictional characters, even if their pleasures are largely less sinful than those that tempt Hercules. Northrop Frye liked to point out that writers often write and rewrite the same myth throughout their careers. 'The Choice of Hercules' is that myth for Johnson. He rewrote it also in 'The Vision of Theodore, the Hermit of Teneriffe'. One of the best essays ever written on Johnson, Lawrence Lipking's 'Learning to Read Johnson: "The Vision of Theodore" and *The Vanity of Human Wishes*', shows the similarities of these works and their mutual centrality in the myth that Johnson was always rewriting.[2]

Johnson pays special attention to the wishes of students in the *Vanity*, but 'The Vision of Theodore' is entirely devoted to the wish for education because it serves as an epilogue to Robert Dodsley's educational textbook *The Preceptor*. Like *Rasselas* and the many oriental tales that Johnson composed in his periodical writings, 'The Vision of Theodore' is presented as an analogue to the wisdom literature of the Bible. The opening addresses the reader as a seeker: 'Son of Perseverance, whoever thou art, whose curiosity has led thee hither, read and be wise' (*Works*, XVI.195). The speaker is the Hermit himself, a kind of prophet, and he recounts a dream vision that came to him in his forty-eighth year. Johnson was thirty-eight when he wrote this, but as in the *Rambler*, he adopted the voice of an elder. In the Hermit's dream he sees 'the Mountain of Existence' with pilgrims labouring up its slopes. At first, the pilgrims are guided by the allegorical figure of Innocence, but when they begin their journey in earnest they are led by Education, 'a nymph more severe in her aspect and imperious in her commands' (XVI.199). As they climb higher, the pilgrims, or students, come under the tutelage of Reason and Religion. Reason in this myth cooperates with Religion and advises students to become her votaries; there is no antagonism between the two, as there came to be for 'freethinkers' around this time. When the students arrive at the top of the Mountain of Existence, Reason can no longer guide them. Those who ascend from the mists of Existence and reach Happiness 'were seen only by the eye of Religion, and though Reason looked after them with the most earnest curiosity, she could only obtain a faint glimpse, when her mistress, to enlarge her prospect, raised her from the ground. Reason however, discerned that they were safe, but Religion saw that they were happy' (*Works*, XVI.209).

The journey, however, is not easy, and many pilgrims fall by the wayside. They are led astray by Appetite and Passion, sometimes thrown from a precipice by Ambition or sunk in gulfs by Intemperance. Complicating the journey are feral, insidious creatures called Habits. These can grow to immense proportions and chain their victims to the most destructive Passions and Appetites, but if they are tamed by Reason, they can contribute to the progress of a student to the realms of Happiness.

The presence of the Habits especially marks this version of Johnson's central myth as autobiographical. His struggle to develop good habits is chronicled in his diaries, prayers, and annals: he constantly admonishes himself, for example, to 'rise early'. He was often beset by passions and appetites; he evidently could not drink moderately, for example, and had to forgo alcohol altogether to avoid the 'gulf of Intemperance'. He even thought of his constitutional melancholy as a habit; he was half-thinking of the old meaning of the word as the chemical balance of the body (its *hexis*, as the Greeks would say), but the modern meaning was certainly in his mind too.

Rasselas

There are also autobiographical elements in Johnson's longest, most popular, and most important fiction, *Rasselas*, even though this work is very much a part of Johnson's professional output rather than an act of personal expression. On 20 January 1759, he told his printer and de facto banker William Strahan that he was preparing for the press a work called 'The choice of Life'; the book eventually came out in April. He made it clear that he needed the money, and he specified three alternative terms of sale to Strahan, saying in a postscript, 'Get me the money if you can' (*Letters*, I.178–9). In the end Strahan, Dodsley, and Johnston became the publishers, paying Johnson £100 for the copyright and another £25 for the second edition.

Johnson knew from the outset roughly what he would write. His oriental tales in the *Rambler*, particularly the story of Seged (a ruler with a scheme of happiness) in numbers 204–5, were good preparation, as was his translation of Father Lobo's *Itinerario*, which took place in the same geographical setting as the new book. Johnson could write such a work 'on demand', but he infused it, as he did all his works, with elements of personal expression.

The premise is quite simple. The Abyssinian prince, Rasselas, becomes discontented with his idyllic existence in the Happy Valley, the place where the royalty of his country are reared. The cause of his discontent is, he says, 'That I want nothing ... or that I know not what I want' (*Works*, XVI.15). In discussion with his old tutor, he settles on wanting to see 'the miseries of the world' because seeing them is necessary to happiness (16).

Rasselas considers various ways to escape from the Happy Valley – including, on the advice of an 'aeronautic projector', by air. On the projector's logic, 'He that can swim needs not despair to fly: to swim is to fly in a grosser fluid, and to fly is to swim in a subtler' (24–5). As usual in Johnson's fictional worlds, as in his non-fictional worlds, theory comes crashing down in the face of experience. After a year spent in preparing his equipment, the projector 'waved his pinions a while to gather air, then leaped from his stand, and in an instant dropped into the lake' (28).

The gently comic mode of *Rasselas* – so different from the violent world of Voltaire's *Candide*, to which it has been so frequently compared – dictates that no harm comes to the hopeful flier: 'His wings, which were of no use in the air, sustained him in the water' (28). Eventually the Prince, along with his sister Nekayah and her maid Pekuah, and the wise tutor Imlac, escape through diligent digging into the mountain. The lesson, which Imlac draws, is as clear and as elementary as those in 'The Vision of Theodore' or a biblical parable: 'Great Works are performed, not by strength, but by perseverance ... He that shall walk with vigour three hours a day will pass in seven years a space equal to the circumference of the globe' (58).

Imlac, a scholar and poet who has already seen the world, has sometimes been taken as an autobiographical figure, like Mr Rambler. The construction of Johnson as sage is one that was encouraged by his conversational aptitude for aphorism; his dictatorial manner; his occasionally severe judgements; and the LLD that allowed Boswell and others to call him 'Dr Johnson'. Johnson was, like Imlac, a scholar and a poet, but in 1759 he had hardly seen the world, and he was certainly not, like Imlac, a retiree.

Much of *Rasselas* is merely episodic. After meeting Imlac and hearing about his inconclusive travels, his inconclusive attempts at poetry, and so on, the Prince meets people in various walks of life and finds them all unhappy, or at least not happy. Hermits are not happy; the poor are not happy; the rich are not happy; 'marriage has many pains, but celibacy has no pleasures' (99); pastoral life is no better than city life.

Rasselas also meets some people who claim to have found the answer to life. One propounds the view that living according to nature is best. Asked what this means, he answers, 'To live according to nature, is to act always with due regard to the fitness arising from the relations and qualities of causes and effects; to concur with the great and unchangeable scheme of universal felicity; to co-operate with the general disposition and tendency of the present system of things' (88). For Rasselas and, it appears, for Johnson, this is a form of cant, a superficially plausible but actually meaningless concatenation of words.

Another philosopher in *Rasselas* is a kind of Stoic. He preaches conquest of the passions, offering 'many examples of heroes immoveable by pain or pleasure' (72–3). Rasselas is enthralled, and though Imlac warns him against disappointment, he goes back to pledge himself to this Stoical path. He finds, however, that the philosopher is in despair over the loss of his daughter and no appeal to philosophy can console him. 'What comfort', he cries, 'can truth and reason afford me?' (75–6). The message again is that there is no simple solution to life's most pressing concerns.

There has been much consternation about the meaning of the ending of *Rasselas*, chapter 49, 'The conclusion, in which nothing is concluded.' In this chapter each of the principal characters forms a wish: Pekuah to be a prioress in the convent of St Anthony; Nekayah 'to found a college of learned women'; the Prince to administer a 'little kingdom'. Imlac and the Astronomer, another sage picked up along the way and restored to mental health by good fellowship, are 'contented to be driven along the stream of life without directing their course to any particular port'. However, not even the wish for desultory experience is granted: 'of these wishes that they had formed they well knew that none could be obtained. They deliberated a while what was to be done, and resolved, when the [annual] inundation [of the Nile] should cease, to return to Abyssinia' (175–6).

Rambler 2 notes that 'The natural flights of the human mind are not from pleasure to pleasure, but from hope to hope' (*Works*, III.10). All human wishes are vain, yet nothing is more human than wishing. *Rasselas* is in effect a mock book of wisdom, a book that refuses to tell one where happiness is to be found and tends to imply that the here and now is good enough. Get used to it. In that respect, *Rasselas* resembles its more violent and bitter cousin, *Candide*, published in the same year. *Rasselas* is also akin to some works of Samuel Beckett, who was a great admirer of Johnson – though Beckett, like Voltaire, had a crueller view of life. A recent book that reinscribes the message of *Rasselas* with less cruelty is Anthony Doerr's *Cloud Cuckoo Land*. There is a class of such books, and *Rasselas* is perhaps its most notable member.

Johnson does not attempt to Christianize *Rasselas* as obviously as he does his great imitation of Juvenal 10. He does something similar, however, by placing the penultimate chapter in the Egyptian catacombs and making this visit to the underworld an occasion for contemplating the nature of the soul. There is little trouble arriving at the understanding that the soul is immaterial, but immateriality itself is above human understanding: 'Of immateriality', said Imlac, 'our ideas are negative and therefore obscure' (172).

Finally, there comes the disturbing question of the soul's durability: 'That it will not perish by any inherent cause of decay, or principle of corruption, may be shown by philosophy; but philosophy can tell no more. That it will not be annihilated by him that made it, we must humbly learn from higher authority' (174). Imlac, in effect, like 'The Vision of Theodore', hands our Pilgrims off from the direction of Education and Reason to the guidance of Religion. The ending therefore of *Rasselas* is neither nihilistic nor existentialist so much as it is a recursion to the old humanist trope that an acceptance of one's ignorance is a mark of wisdom.

Interpreters of Johnson's meaning should probably be warned, however, against placing too much emphasis on the endings of even his most important works, *Rasselas* and the *Vanity of Human Wishes*. Johnson criticized Shakespeare for neglecting 'the latter part' of his plays: 'When he found himself near the end of his work, and in view of his reward, he shortened the labour, to snatch the profit' (*Works*, VII.72–3). When he said this in 1765, Johnson may also have been thinking of himself. He ended his public performances when he had fulfilled his contract and not necessarily when he had found the most satisfying conclusion. As A, B, and C are proportionately the longest parts of Johnson's *Dictionary*, X, Y, Z are the shortest: this is an algorithm that applies, to some degree, to all of Johnson's works.

Chapter 4

Scholar

> Literature. *n.s.* [*literatura*, Lat.] Learning; skill in letters.
> (*Dictionary*)

The eccentric but deeply learned schoolmaster Dr Samuel Parr, known as the Whig Dr Johnson, despised Boswell's *Life of Johnson* and planned his own: 'Mine', he said, 'should have been, not the droppings of his lips, but the history of his mind.'[1] Like most of Parr's projects, this one was never executed, but in his judgement, 'Dr Johnson was an admirable scholar; and would have had high reputation for mere learning, if his reputation for intellect and eloquence had not overshadowed it.' Parr's only lasting contribution to Johnson's reputation is the epitaph he composed for the monumental statue in St Paul's, but his estimate of Johnson as a scholar should not be forgotten.

Johnson's education, beginning at the Lichfield Grammar School, prepared him for a life of scholarship focused on classical learning. Like other schoolboys of his time – and any time after the reign of Elizabeth – Johnson studied classical grammar and was initiated into the tenets of humanism that had been established by Erasmus and Dean Colet in England two centuries earlier. The importance of studying languages, particularly classical Latin and Greek, is a key tenet of humanism. Emphasis on the Latin of Augustan Rome freed learning from medieval Latin and, as some humanists saw it, the superstition of the Roman Catholic Church. The close textual analysis of Virgil, Cicero, and Horace as well as the Bible was both an intellectual and a religious commitment, and the great humanist scholars who pioneered such study were Johnson's heroes throughout his life: Erasmus, Roger Ascham, Angelo Poliziano, Pico della Mirandola, Pontano, Melanchthon. Such scholars haunt the pages of Johnson's writing. Above all, he admired Joseph Scaliger, who excelled as a poet, a textual critic, a lexicographer, and a chronologer in a work that combined all his studies, *De Emendatione Temporum* (*On the Correct Chronology of Events in the Ancient World*).

Unlike Swift and Pope, Johnson was not often satirical about true scholarship. He was in this regard, as in others, more like Addison, who could have led a happy academic life at Magdalen College, Oxford, had he not been drawn into public service. Johnson had, for example, a high regard for Richard Bentley, the butt of so much humour by the Scriblerians but a brilliant editor of classical texts. Johnson wrote plenty of intellectual satire, of course, but only unelevated, materialistic kinds of scholarship – antiquarian collecting, for example – or cloistered, uncommunicated scholarship like Thomas Gray's drew his scorn.

If Johnson had been a trust-fund baby, things might have been different, but he had to put earning a living ahead of his desire for pure scholarship. He tried to combine the two when, shortly after leaving college, he proposed to edit the poetry of the Renaissance humanist Angelo Poliziano and join the ranks of neo-Latin scholar-poets; but his proposals for that work fell flat. He also failed to find steady work as a teacher, which would have been another sort of compromise between scholarship and financial stability. The more productive compromise he made, as he set off for London in 1737, was to write scholarly works in English, which would reach a larger audience and therefore be remunerative. His first successful proposal to Edward Cave at the *Gentleman's Magazine* was to translate Paolo Sarpi's *History of the Council of Trent*, an important work in church history by a significant early modern scholar. This work was never finished, but Johnson was soon writing biographies of great scholars, as well as translations. He gradually turned to writing scholarly works of his own, albeit only in English.

Johnson never regarded his translations or his English works as approaching the dignity of the great works of European humanism, but we know them now as major feats of scholarship in their own right. The *Dictionary of the English Language* (1755) and *The Plays of William Shakespeare* (1765) are his most important scholarly works – scholarly in the traditional, humanistic sense that they are primarily philological. His edition of Roger Ascham's *English Works* and of Thomas Browne's *Christian Morals* also qualify to a degree, as does some of Johnson's poetry – notably his translations into Latin of many Greek epigrams from the *Greek Anthology* – parts of many of his biographies, and his bibliographical work on the Catalogue of the Harleian Library. In an *Introduction* to Johnson's works, however, the *Dictionary* and *The Plays of Shakespeare* must take precedence.

Before the *Dictionary*

Johnson suspended much of his journalistic activity in the period 1742–4 to work on the catalogue of the great Harleian Library. The whole library was estimated to contain 300,000 items. Johnson's task excluded the manuscripts, which ended up in the King's Library and formed the basis of the British Library when it opened in 1752; the prints and drawings were also set aside. But that still left hundreds of thousands of books and pamphlets for Johnson and Edward Harley's former secretary, William Oldys, to work over and describe in the five volumes of the sale catalogue. Johnson's attention sometimes wandered beyond the title pages and colophons; as the story goes, the bookseller Thomas Osborne berated him for wasting time in reading – whereupon Johnson felled him with a folio, as one of his idols, the great humanist Poggio Bracciolini, had felled an adversary three centuries earlier. Johnson denied doing more than correcting the man's insolence (*Miscellanies*, I.304), but the point is that this scholarly activity – this immersion in books – immediately preceded Johnson's engagement in his greatest scholarly projects and probably supplied him with some of the books he needed to perform them.

Serial publication of the last Harleian project – an eight-volume collection of its rare pamphlets – began in March 1744. Within months, Johnson was at work on Shakespeare. In 1745, he published proposals for a ten-volume edition and provided, as a specimen or teaser, *Miscellaneous Observations on the Tragedy of Macbeth*. This work shows Johnson at the most antiquarian phase of his scholarly life. Partly due to the subject of *Macbeth*, Johnson's notes involve him in Saxon etymologies, Thomas Hearne's medieval studies, and the obscure figure of Hanvil the Monk. This immersion in northern or Gothic learning was not part of traditional humanism, and it represented a departure for Johnson.

Johnson's initial approach to Shakespeare had to be set aside because of legal wrangling among London publishers, but he continued his work on Shakespeare as he began the greatest project of his life; so his two greatest scholarly works became intertwined. In 1746, the London publishers approached Johnson to compile *A Dictionary of the English Language* to rival the great national dictionaries of France and Italy. That those were produced by national academies, whereas this would be the work of an individual, was a point of pride from the start. Garrick provided a distich: 'And Johnson, well arm'd like a hero of yore,/ Has beat forty French, and will beat forty more!' (*Life*, I.301). The full story came from an old Pembroke man, Dr Adams, who says he asked Johnson how he expected to produce in three years (as he first planned) a work that took forty French academicians forty years: 'Sir, thus it is. This is the proportion. Let me see; forty times forty is sixteen hundred. As three to sixteen hundred, so is the proportion of an Englishman to a Frenchman' (*Life*, I.186).

A Book Made of Other Books

In the event, it took Johnson nine years to bring the *Dictionary* to press, and he had the help of six amanuenses, but he certainly governed the project and established the methodology – which was scholarly and humanistic, despite the fact that its subject is a 'vulgar' (i.e. modern) language. Like other lexicographers, Johnson used earlier dictionaries: Nathan Baily's *Dictionarium Britannicum* (2nd ed., 1736) was the most important, although there were others, including Edward Phillips's *New World of Words* (6th ed., 1706), and specialized dictionaries for etymology and certain subjects, such as legal and military language. He also used encyclopedias: Ephraim Chambers's *Cyclopedia* (4th ed., 1741) is the most important, but he also used John Harris's *Lexicon Technicum* (5th ed., 1736) and Philip Miller's *Gardeners Dictionary* (3rd ed., 1748), and others. All lexicographers depend on other dictionaries, but most before Johnson relied on them to a greater degree than he did (and, unlike Johnson, they often concealed that reliance).

Johnson's great innovation was that – more than any previous English lexicographer and in the spirit of the humanist lexicographers of Latin – he compiled his dictionary empirically. That is, he read books (mainly those written from the late sixteenth century to the mid eighteenth century) and recorded their usage of English. He went to the source, practising philology by studying the texts themselves and determining the extent and meaning of English words in them. As an example of his normal procedure, here is his entry on 'officious,' a word whose meaning was in transition in Johnson's time:

>OFFI'CIOUS. *adj.*
>[*officieux*, Fr. *officiosus*, Lat.]
>
>1\. Kind; doing good offices.
>>Yet, not to earth are those bright luminaries
>>*Officious;* but to thee, earth's habitant.
>>Milt. P. Lost.
>
>2\. Importunely forward.
>>You are too *officious*
>>In her behalf that scorns your services. *Shakesp.*
>>At Taunton they killed in fury an *officious* and eager commissioner for the subsidy. *Bacon's Henry* VII.
>>Cato, perhaps
>>I'm too *officious,* but my forward cares
>>Would fain preserve a life of so much value.
>>Addison.

Johnson's empirical approach led directly to the *Oxford English Dictionary* (*OED*) of the nineteenth and twentieth centuries.

Groundbreaking as it was, there were limitations to Johnson's empiricism. He did not much consider oral language, and when he did, he tended to brand its usage as 'merely oral'. In the Preface to the *Dictionary*, he explained the view behind this somewhat dismissive phrase:

> As language was at its beginning merely oral, all words of necessary or common use were spoken before they were written; and while they were unfixed by any visible signs, must have been spoken with great diversity, as we now observe those who cannot read to catch sounds imperfectly, and utter them negligently. When this wild and barbarous jargon was first reduced to an alphabet, every penman endeavoured to express, as he could, the sounds which he was accustomed to pronounce or to receive, and vitiated [i.e. corrupted] in writing such words as were already vitiated in speech.   (*Works*, XVIII.75)

Written language is superior in Johnson's view because it is relatively stable, fixed, and refined, whereas oral language, like pronunciation, varies more dramatically from place to place and time to time.

Modern linguists (though not 'grammatologists' like Derrida) take the opposite view and regard oral speech as primary, written as secondary. Johnson, however, is not modern; he is a humanistic philologer focused on books – and mainly printed books, which offer the highest level of linguistic stability. In a poem he composed in 1771 when he was supposed to be listening to Thomas Arne's *Love in a Village,* Johnson described himself as not suited for the pleasures of live performance. He was, rather, an old man happier among books, being studious of truth: 'Codices, veri studiosus inter' (*In Theatro*, l. 10). This was true not only when Johnson was old; for all his love of conversation, his scholarly métier was always books, not living language.

Johnson made his *Dictionary* mainly out of books, but not just any books. Unlike the creators of the *OED*, he largely excluded medieval books – those written before 1500 – and contemporary writers. A few living authors come in, including himself, but, with the exception of Samuel Richardson, whose delineation of moral sentiments was too appealing to ignore, their appearances are scant. Johnson based his *Dictionary* mainly on the works of acknowledged masters of English poetry and prose who were active in less than the previous two centuries. Far from hiding this bias, Johnson explicitly cites his authorities in his treatment of the words he gleaned from their works: this collection of some 113,600 quotations is the most striking feature of his book (he added 2,800 more in 1773). Not surprisingly, Shakespeare is the most frequently quoted writer, accounting for more than 17,000 quotations, about 15 per cent of the total.[2]

This is partly because Johnson was preparing to edit Shakespeare at the same time that he was constructing his *Dictionary*. His copy of Warburton's edition of Shakespeare (seven of the eight volumes are in University College, Aberystwyth) is covered with the markings Johnson used before passing his books on to his amanuenses for copying: vertical lines surround the passage to be copied, the word of interest is underlined, and its initial is written in the margin.

Other writers who are very prominent in the *Dictionary*'s illustrative quotations include Milton (7,000), Dryden (12,000), Addison (4,600), Pope (4,200), Bacon (5,000), Locke (3,300), Swift (3,300), and Hooker (2,200). All told, these famous writers account for almost half of the quotations in the book. When one adds to that the 4,500 biblical citations and all the quotations from dictionaries and encyclopedias, one can see that Johnson did not leave much room for the full range of English usage available to him.

The English captured in Johnson's *Dictionary* is, with few exceptions, an elite English written from the time of Shakespeare to the death of Swift in 1745. It is also English English, with only rare exceptions: for example, a few Scots or Scots-English words come in, sometimes through the good offices of Johnson's amanuenses, five of whom were Scottish. Many of these appear in etymologies, however, rather than as headwords. Other sorts of regional English are also rare, although Johnson consulted some works with regional vocabulary – such as Richard Carew's *Survey of Cornwall*, which supplied him with a handful of words (e.g. 'huer', 'balkers', and 'blobber'). He could also add personal knowledge of a regionalism, as when he noted that in Staffordshire a goldfinch is called a 'proud taylor'. Such appearances are rare, however, and most of the unusual, archaic, or regional words come in only if they happen to be used by a standard author, such as Shakespeare or Spenser. Even then, they may not appear. 'Aroint', for example, which occurs in *Macbeth* (I.iii.6) and draws a long comment in Johnson's 1745 proposal for his edition of Shakespeare, does not have a place as a headword in the *Dictionary*.

'A Wretched Etymologist'

The etymologies provide the richest representation of archaic or non-standard English in the *Dictionary* and the largest number of Saxon or Gothic words – outside, that is, of the 'History of the English Language' that Johnson prefixed to the *Dictionary*. It is important to note that Johnson's

'History' is the largest selection of Old English that had ever been printed in a standard reference work up to that time. Much of the proper Old English comes from Hickes's *Thesaurus*, which Johnson encountered and perhaps acquired in the Harleian Library. The transcriptions of Old English, however, show that Johnson did not read that language well, or perhaps (which may imply the same thing) did not proofread the transcriptions. Moreover, the 'History' moves into early modern English fairly quickly and prints as much from Sir Thomas More, a humanist author of particular interest to Johnson, as it does from Old English texts.

The etymologies are generally considered the worst part of Johnson's *Dictionary*. Macaulay was not altogether wrong when he wrote: 'Johnson was a wretched etymologist. He knew little or nothing of any Teutonic language except English, which indeed, as he wrote it, was scarcely a Teutonic language; and thus he was absolutely at the mercy of Junius and Skinner.'[3] Franciscus Junius and Stephen Skinner are the respective authors of the etymological dictionaries Johnson most cited. He followed them, for the most part, but not uncritically. In his Preface he especially criticized the theory of etymology in Junius, which tends to assume that all languages are connected in literal ways, so that he can derive 'dream' from the unrelated Greek 'drama', 'action', because the words sound alike and he can make them both relate to the genre of comedy.

Johnson has been much ridiculed for his etymology of 'spider', which mocks Junius but then comes up with something similarly fanciful:

> *Skinner* thinks this word softened from *spinder*, or *spinner*, from *spin*: *Junius*, with his usual felicity, dreams that it comes from *spizein* [Greek] to extend; for the spider extends his web. Perhaps it comes from *spieden*, Dutch; *speyden*, Danish, to spy, to lye upon the catch. *Dor, Dora*, Saxon, is a *beetle*, or properly an *humble bee*, or *stingless bee*. May not *spider* be *spy dor*, the insect that watches the *dor*?

Skinner, as usual, is closer to the truth than Junius. At least Johnson sees that the word is Anglo-Saxon, and he is right about the origin of 'spy' and the meaning of *dor*. Often when this story is told, *dor* is assumed to be 'door'. Johnson was not that ill-informed.

For all its Saxonic touches, Johnson's *Dictionary* still is a Renaissance humanist tome in the main. Johnson realizes that English is a Germanic language, but he presents a largely refined form of English. It is not truly Latinate, but it leans southward, as the vast number of Latin etymologies show. There are plenty of French etymologies too, but not as many as there should be, and there is a resistance to what he laments as the 'Gallic' element in English.

'Interspersions of Morality'

The humanism of the *Dictionary* is evident in its conception of language, but it is also evident in the way it constantly reinforces the humanistic tenet that learning language should be coextensive with learning religion and morality. In his definition of 'crossrow', Johnson articulated this basic humanistic tenet succinctly: 'Alphabet; so named because a cross is placed at the beginning, to shew that the end of learning is piety.' Johnson directed the reader towards piety in various ways. Most importantly, he chose his illustrative quotations from many books filled with moral and religious sentiments. Under the word 'philology', he quotes William Walker, *English Examples of the Latine Syntaxis* (1683): 'Temper all discourses of *philology* with interspersions of morality.' Johnson follows this humanistic rule to a 'T'.

Even for the language of science – or natural philosophy, as it was then called – he chose books written on the principle that nature is a standing revelation of God's providential power. Johnson often quotes John Ray's book *The Wisdom of God Manifested in the Works of Creation* (1691). This approach to science was called physico-theology, and a book of that name by William Derham caught Johnson's attention for this project: *Physico-Theology: or a Demonstration of the Being and Attributes of God from His Works of Creation* (1714).

Many quotations from the physico-theologists have nothing to do with religion: Derham's remark under 'crab' – 'the fox catches *crab* fish with his tail' – does not instil religion. But if we consult the *Dictionary* on, say, the word 'incurious', we read Derham saying: 'The Creator did not bestow so much skill upon his creatures, to be looked upon with a careless *incurious* eye.'

Johnson also introduced religious sentiments more directly, by quoting volumes of sermons by numerous bishops of the Church of England such as Robert South, John Tillotson, and Edward Stillingfleet. In choosing religious writers, on the whole Johnson stayed away from non-jurors and non-conformists; some of his favourites among those appear too – such as Isaac Watts and John Calamy – but their subversive views are not quoted. Moreover, some theologically unorthodox writers are excluded from the *Dictionary*. Hobbes is banned, while his adversary John Bramhall gets a considerable amount of ink; Samuel Clarke, much as Johnson admired him as a scholar, cannot get more than a word in edgewise because he was notoriously 'weak on the Trinity'. Johnson read Clarke and many other heterodox writers himself, but he did not want implicitly to recommend them to his audience by quoting them lavishly in the *Dictionary*.

Definitions

> Definition is not the Province of Man
> (*Rambler* 125, *Works*, IV.300)

The vast sea of illustrative quotations in Johnson's *Dictionary* reveals much about his reading, his scholarship, and his intentions for his great book, but everyone's favourite parts of the *Dictionary* are the definitions. Here, Johnson could most employ his literary gifts, though he also shows his humanistic learning because his definitions often hint at the Latin roots of English words. For example, 'seminary' is 'Breeding place; place of education, from whence scholars are transplanted into life' – reminding us that the word comes from the Latin *semen*, seed. Similarly, 'terrier' is a 'dog that follows his game underground' because the word comes from Latin, *terra*, meaning ground or earth.

These Latinate definitions are part of a broader intention in the *Dictionary* to tie all words – regardless of their language of origin – to what Johnson calls their 'primitive' meanings. In the Preface, he explains what he means by this term: 'A primitive word, is that which can be traced no further to any *English* root' (*Works*, XVIII.80).

When defining words of 'extensive use', Johnson wished 'to mark the progress of its meaning, and show by what gradations of intermediate sense it has passed from its primitive to its remote and accidental signification; so that every foregoing explanation should tend to that which follows, and the series be regularly concatenated from the first notion to the last' (91). He admits that such an approach is

> not always practicable; kindred senses may be so interwoven, that the perplexity cannot be disentangled, nor any reason be assigned why one should be ranged before the other. When the radical idea branches out into parallel ramifications, how can a consecutive series be formed of senses in their nature collateral? The shades of meaning sometimes pass imperceptibly into each other; so that though on one side they apparently differ, yet it is impossible to mark the point of contact.

Nevertheless, he tries. So, under 'to break' he says, 'It is to be observed of this extensive and perplexed *verb*, that, in all its significations, whether *active* or *neutral* [transitive or intransitive], it has some reference to its primitive meaning, by implying either detriment, suddenness or violence'. Here and elsewhere when dealing with common words, the breadth of the semantic field strains even Johnson's powers of generalization.

Connecting words to their primitive meaning – and even believing that there is a primitive meaning – is a kind of philosophy of language. Johnson follows this philosophy in arranging his definitions, but often it is, as he said, 'impracticable' or irrelevant. On some of these occasions, his attempts at clarification produce ludicrous results. 'To roll', for example, is, unhelpfully, 'To move any thing by volutation, or successive application of the different parts of the surface, to the ground.' 'Net', in Johnson's revision of 1773, is 'Any thing made with interstitial vacuities.' 'To sip' is equally ludicrous but strikingly accurate: 'To drink by small draughts; to take at one apposition of the cup to the mouth no more than the mouth will contain.' The prize for confusing explanation, however, goes to 'Touch': 'Reach of anything so that there is no space between the things reaching and the reached.'

A less philosophical way that Johnson deals with definition is through a burst of synonyms. These sound at times like emotional responses to a word. For example, 'To Perplex' is 'To disturb with doubtful notions; to entangle; to make anxious; to teaze with suspense or ambiguity; to distract; to embarrass; to puzzle.' The definition imitates the meaning of the word. One could say the same about 'To Plague': 'To trouble; to teaze; to vex; to harrass; to torment; to afflict; to distress; to torture; to embarrass; to excruciate; to make uneasy; to disturb.'

Sometimes, Johnson's synonymy also seems to express his basic pessimism or other personal attitudes. A 'Winner' is simply 'One who wins', whereas a 'Loser' is 'One that is deprived of any thing; one that forfeits any thing; one that is impaired in his possession or hope: the contrary to *winner* or *gainer*'. There is an autobiographical element in Johnson's scholarship, even at the most molecular level, and the autobiography is usually lugubrious.

A Harmless Drudge

Perhaps the most famous parts of Johnson's *Dictionary*, though they are a very small part of the whole, are the moments of personal expression. He famously defines 'lexicographer' as 'a harmless drudge' and, though he excluded proper names from the *Dictionary*, he makes an exception for 'Lichfield', echoing Virgil as he writes, 'Salve magna parens' ('Hail, great mother'). 'Grubstreet', his other home, is another exception: 'Originally the name of a street in Moorfields in London, much inhabited by writers of small histories, dictionaries, and temporary poems; whence any mean production is called *grubstreet*.'

Such humour seems to us quintessentially Johnsonian, but the self-denigrating (or self-aggrandizing) jest is part of the humanistic tradition of scholarship. The joke about Grubstreet belongs to the tradition of jokes about scholars in *The Jests of Hierocles* or Erasmus's *Encomium Morae*, meaning the praise both of folly and of his friend Thomas More. Like the multilingual puns in Milton, the Greek insertion (see p. 26 above) is written not for the public – the main audience of the *Dictionary* – but for the fraternity of scholars to which Johnson always belonged.

Shakespeare at Last

By the time he finished the *Dictionary*, Johnson was in good shape to edit Shakespeare. He had read the plays carefully and studied their vocabulary. Almost immediately, he reissued his proposals, but the need to keep earning money kept him from the project for another few years. During that time he composed most of the articles for the *Literary Magazine* (1756–7); wrote the *Idler* (1760–2); edited Sir Thomas Browne (1756) and Roger Ascham (1761); and did all kinds of literary piecework – dedications for friends, introductions for publishers, and letters for the Society of Artists. As a result, he did not finish the project until 1765, three years after he received his pension from George III.

Editing was arguably the primary activity of humanist scholars. Sound editing practically defined humanism, but it was traditionally aimed only at classical texts. Only gradually did the practice extend to works in modern languages. Alexander Pope edited Shakespeare in a light, gentlemanly, but intelligent way; others, such as William Warburton, did a more thorough scholarly job. Milton, too, had been edited – by the great scholar Richard Bentley, but more sensibly by Thomas Newton, who rejected Bentley's proposed emendations.

'I Have Rescued Many Lines'

The two main parts of scholarly editing are the establishment of the text, and the commentary. Johnson's textual scholarship on Shakespeare was forward-looking: he was more inclined than his predecessors to trust the early editions and less inclined to substitute readings of the text that seemed 'better' (more sensible, more literate, more 'Shakespearean'). As he put it in the Preface, 'I have rescued many lines from the violations of temerity' (*Works*, VII.106).

Johnson did occasionally propose imaginative emendations, as humanist critics before him had done, but he was cautious and kept his suggestions to the foot rather than the fore of the page (as in fact the great Bentley had done in his Milton edition). The Preface summed up his textual-critical principles:

> Conjecture, though it be sometimes unavoidable, I have not wantonly nor licentiously indulged. It has been my settled principle, that the reading of the ancient books [the early folios and quartos] is probably true, and therefore is not to be disturbed for the sake of elegance, perspicuity, or mere improvement of the sense. For though much credit is not due to the fidelity, nor any to the judgement of the first publishers, yet they who had the copy before their eyes were more likely to read it right, than we who read it only by imagination. But it is evident that they have often made strange mistakes by ignorance or negligence, and that therefore something may be properly attempted by criticism, keeping the middle way between presumption and timidity.   (*Works*, VII.106)

Before leaving the subject of textual criticism, Johnson cites some of his humanist heroes – Scaliger, Salmasius, Huet, and Lipsius – warning against the folly of over-zealous emendation. Although his subject is a modern author, Johnson is trying to be a critic on the model of the humanists who edited Greek and Latin manuscripts.

Nevertheless, Johnson does want Shakespeare to make sense, and sense for Johnson is often moral sense. In *Macbeth* V.v, for example, Johnson reacts to the passage in which Macbeth, having heard of his wife's death, makes this famous speech:

> She should have died hereafter;
> There would have been a time for such a *word*,
> To-morrow, and to-morrow, and to-morrow
> Creeps in this petty pace from day to day,
> To the last syllable of recorded time;
> And all our yesterdays have lighted fools
> The way to dusty death. Out, out, brief candle!
> Life's but a walking shadow.
>
> [Italics in Johnson's citation]

Johnson thinks 'word' is a mistake for 'world', and in his note he paraphrases the passage, drawing attention to the moral:

> Such is the *world* – such is the condition of human life, that we always think *to-morrow* will be happier than to-day, but to-morrow and to-morrow steals over us unenjoyed and unregarded, and we still linger in the same expectation to the moment appointed for our end. All these days, which have thus passed away, have sent multitudes of fools to the grave, who were engrossed by the same dream of future felicity, and,

when life was departing from them, were like me reckoning on tomorrow. (*Works*, VII.41–42)

A passage that makes sense to Johnson is one that reiterates the message of his great poem, the *Vanity of Human Wishes*, and as a humanistic scholar, Johnson is both philologer and moralist.

Most of the time, it should be said, Johnson resists emendation of this conjectural sort. In *Othello* III.i, for example, Othello says:

> 'Tis not to make me jealous,
> To say, my wife is fair, feeds well, loves company,
> Is free of speech, sings, plays, and dances well;
> Where virtue is, these are most virtuous.

Johnson attaches Warburton's emendation of the last line from his edition of 1747: '[Warburton: these make more virtuous]'. Then he adds, 'The old reading will, I think, approve itself to every understanding that has not an interest in changing it. An action in itself "indifferent", grows "virtuous" by its end and application' (*Works*, VIII.1032).

Interestingly, in the second edition of his Shakespeare (1773) Johnson removed Warburton's remark, and the first sentence of his comment. He had become a bit less harshly critical of his predecessors. Perhaps he had mellowed, although sharp rejoinders to other critics are very much in the spirit of the old humanists he admired.

Johnson's textual criticism is smart and interesting, but it must be confessed that he was not as thorough as possible in collating the early printings and sticking to the professional task. He probably did not look at a First Folio, though he had opportunities to do so. He sometimes refers vaguely to 'one of the folio editions' (e.g. VIII.757), as though he had seen but not collated them. Johnson did what he could with his wits and the resources that he could easily gather. The case is similar in other research projects in his life. He eschewed research in the British Museum for his *Lives of the Poets*, for example, and sent Hester Thrale Piozzi and James Boswell to make some transcriptions. He summed up his attitude at about that time (1778) when he told Boswell, 'If it rained knowledge I'd hold out my hand; but I would not give myself the trouble to go in quest of it' (*Life*, III.344).

'The Mind Is Refrigerated by Interruption'

In addition to textual notes, of course, Johnson wrote a great many explanatory notes or comments in his edition of Shakespeare. He made a wonderful remark about notes of this kind in his Preface (a work treated more fully as part of Johnson's literary criticism in Chapter 5):

> Notes are often necessary, but they are necessary evils. Let him, that is yet unacquainted with the powers of Shakespeare, and who desires to feel the highest pleasure that the drama can give, read every play from the first scene to the last, with utter negligence of all his commentators ... Let him read on through brightness and obscurity, through integrity and corruption; let him preserve his comprehension of the dialogue and his interest in the fable. ... The mind is refrigerated by interruption; the thoughts are diverted from the principal subject; the reader is weary, he suspects not why; and at last throws away the book, which he has too diligently studied. (*Works*, VII.111)

For all his mistrust of footnotes, Johnson excelled at writing them, and he put his stamp on them both stylistically and thematically. He knew the form well not only from his study of scholarly editions of classical texts but also from his flirtation with an antiquarian form of scholarship in his earlier days. His notes on books in the Harleian Catalogue are basically footnotes, for example, and his life of the Earl of Roscommon appeared in the *Gentleman's Magazine* with a proportion of about 4:1 of notes to text. This unusual form has prompted some critics to speculate that he had initially prepared the biography (1748) for Thomas Birch's edition of *Biographica Britannica* (1747–66). One of Johnson's most important early contacts in London, Birch was an antiquarian who might have been a model for Johnson before he committed himself to a more popular mode of literary endeavour.

Birch, who received pre-publication copies of Johnson's *Dictionary* and his Shakespeare, reacted to Johnson's works as old-fashioned scholarly projects of the kind Birch himself knew well. In fact, he wrote seventy-three pages in his notebooks on Johnson's edition, most of them devoted to Johnson's treatment of earlier editors.[4] Johnson's edition was the first 'variorum'-style edition, providing in its notes a history of the commentary on Shakespeare as well as new interpretations. He was not as exhaustive as the *Variorum Shakespeare* begun in the nineteenth century by Frederick James Furnivall, but he established the prototype. In the Yale edition of Johnson's Shakespeare most of this commentary had to be sacrificed to bring the work down from its original eight to a mere two volumes: Johnson's own comments are preserved, including those on earlier editors, but the edition only retains as much of their work as is required for understanding Johnson's comments. This abbreviation gives the impression that Johnson's Shakespeare is a less antiquarian work than it is. Arguably, Birch saw it more accurately.

Johnson's comments themselves sometimes amount to short essays, miniature versions of his *Ramblers*. In his Preface, Johnson says Shakespeare's greatest fault was that he failed in a 'writer's duty to make the world better', not making clear his disapprobation of evil. In general, 'He sacrifices virtue to convenience, and is so much more careful to please than to instruct, that he seems to write without any moral purpose' (*Works*, VII.71). The best and most Johnsonian of Johnson's notes attempt to remedy this situation by drawing out the moral implications of Shakespeare's lines. Some of these notes resemble his proposed emendation of 'world' for 'word', just discussed; at other times, there is no editorial pretext for a moment of moralizing or generalizing.

To take a small example, in *2 Henry IV*, IV.iii.86, Falstaff says, 'Good faith, this same young sober-blooded boy doth not love me; nor a man cannot make him laugh.' Johnson comments, without any textual issue at stake: 'Falstaff speaks here like a veteran of life. The young prince did not love him, and he despaired to gain his affection, for he could not make him laugh. Men only become friends by community of pleasures. He who cannot be softened into gayety cannot easily be melted into kindness' (*Works*, VII.513).

Examples of Johnson supplementing the incomplete moral lessons of Shakespeare can be found throughout his edition. They are not as frequent as the compressed Yale edition makes them seem, but they are characteristic of his scholarship and not uncommon. At *Othello*, III.iii.210, for example, Iago says, 'She did deceive her father, marrying you;/ And when she seem'd to shake, and fear your looks,/ She lov'd them most.' Johnson comments at length:

> This and the following argument of Iago ought to be deeply impressed on every reader. Deceit and falsehood, whatever conveniences they may for a time promise or produce, are, in the sum of life, obstacles to happiness. Those who profit by the cheat, distrust the deceiver, and the act by which kindness was sought, puts an end to confidence.
>
> The same objection may be made with a lower degree of strength against the imprudent generosity of disproportionate marriages. When the first heat of passion is over, it is easily succeeded by suspicion, that the same violence of inclination which caused one irregularity, may stimulate to another; and those who have shewn, that their passions are too powerful for their prudence, will, with very slight appearances against them, be censured, as not very likely to restrain them by their virtue. (*Works*, VIII.1032–3)

For a modern Shakespearean, Johnson's note appears to make Shakespeare into a novelist on the model of Samuel Richardson. For Johnson, however, a modern, formalist critic – conscious of ambiguity and 'negative capability' in Shakespeare – would deprive the Bard of the true moral force of literature, which the humanists knew so well. Johnson might in fact be more receptive to recent cultural, post-colonial readings of Shakespeare, as long as they were sufficiently general, and therefore truly moral.

Johnson's commentary is scholarly, and it puts Shakespeare in a scholarly tradition, but the aim is always moral education. Under 'to learn' in his *Dictionary*, Johnson misquotes Shakespeare so that he has Caliban say to Prospero, 'You taught me language and my profit on't/ Is, I know not how to curse: the red plague rid you,/ For *learning* me your language'. The 'not' is Johnson's interpolation, converting Caliban's anger at his teacher into a summary of proper teaching. Johnson did not emend this passage in his Shakespeare, but he does try to change the way Shakespeare is read, and sometimes this entails invoking the humanistic tradition of commentary on classical works. There is an interesting example at the beginning of *Twelfth Night*. Orsino is lovesick for Olivia and expressing it in metaphysical terms:

> O, when my eyes did see Olivia first,
> Methought, she purg'd the air of pestilence;
> That instant was I turn'd into a hart.

Johnson comments:

> This image evidently alludes to the story of Acteon [in Ovid's *Metamorphoses*], by which Shakespeare seems to think men cautioned against too great familiarity with forbidden beauty. Acteon, who saw Diana naked, and was torn in pieces by his hounds, represents a man, who indulging his eyes, or his imagination, with the view of a woman that he cannot gain, has his heart torn with incessant longing. An interpretation far more elegant and natural than that of Sir Francis Bacon, who, in his *Wisdom of the Antients*, supposes this story to warn us against enquiring into the secrets of princes, by showing, that those who knew that which for reasons of state is to be concealed, will be detected and destroyed by their own servants.   (*Works*, VII.311)

In this note, Johnson sees Shakespeare as a commentator on Ovid, and he aligns himself with his interpretation, as opposed to Bacon's. Although he was editing a popular modern author who wrote in English, rather than a classical author, such as Virgil, or an early modern scion of the classical tradition, such as Poliziano, Johnson nevertheless presented himself as a humanistic scholar.

Know Thyself

Johnson's identification of himself as a scholar – or a scholar *manqué* – was lifelong, but his public production of scholarship waned after he completed his edition of Shakespeare. He was not quite finished in 1765: there was a revised second edition, produced in collaboration with George Steevens, which came out in 1773. At the same time, Johnson revised his *Dictionary*, his other great scholarly project: that revision came out in the same year, the date that marks the end of his public career as a textual scholar.

Also that year, Johnson wrote a Latin poem addressed to the greatest of his humanistic idols, Joseph Scaliger. He gave it a Greek name – Γνῶθι Σεαυτόν (Know Thyself) – the motto said to have been engraved on the temple at Delphi and to contain the sum of wisdom. What Johnson knows about himself in this poem is that he is not as great a scholar as Scaliger and not entitled to complain about the drudgery of lexicography. 'Each man', the poem says, 'should know his limited ability. That I should hope to match you in scholarship, the foremost of men, or dare to match your complaints is denied by fate, whether I am hindered by the chill of sluggish blood or languishing too long in idleness, or because nature has endowed me with an inferior mind' (*LAEP*, 456). This melancholy poem ends with Johnson facing loneliness and inactivity, resolving perhaps to go back to the only sort of activity for which he is good enough – writing dictionary entries or footnotes.

Johnson was a better scholar than most of the great writers in the English tradition, even if he was not up to Scaliger's standard, or the grand level on which Samuel Parr wished to place him. Among major British writers, perhaps only Milton was clearly superior. After the *Dictionary* and Shakespeare were revised, Johnson still wrote a good deal of Latin poetry, including Latin translations of many Greek epigrams and a workmanlike prose translation of Sallust. None of these were published or meant to be published, however, and his last great work, the *Lives of the Poets*, is more a work of reminiscence and critical interpretation than a work of old-fashioned (i.e. textual) scholarship. There are very few footnotes, though the need for them has been amply shown by the great editions of the *Lives*. Such archival material as Johnson presents in the *Lives* was ferreted out for him by Piozzi or Boswell. His scholarly existence after 1773 was largely confined to his private life, but there it never left him.

Chapter 5

Critic

> Judgment, like other faculties, is improved by practice, and its advancement is hindered by submission to dictatorial decisions, as the memory grows torpid by the use of a table book.
> (Preface to Shakespeare, *Works*, VII.104)

Asked why biographies of Johnson have proliferated despite the brilliance of Boswell's masterwork, Harold Bloom gave a simple answer: 'the spiritual complexity and intellectual splendor of the most eminent of all literary critics'.[1] Perhaps it is not surprising that Bloom, an eminent critic himself, should see Johnson primarily in that role, but there is plenty of evidence – apart from Bloom's testimony – that criticism was central to Johnson's enormous intellectual activity. It may surprise us, then, that Johnson did not see criticism in especially exalted terms. In the last *Rambler* (no. 208) he reviewed the subjects he had pursued in the whole series of essays. His 'principal design' was of course 'to inculcate wisdom or piety', and he ranks his performances in ascending order of their contributions to that end. Criticism comes in second in line from the bottom, only ahead of fiction: 'Next to the excursions of fancy are the disquisitions of criticism, which, in my opinion, is only to be ranked among the subordinate and instrumental arts' (*Works*, V.319).

However subordinate, the art of criticism was one which Johnson took seriously. It should, he declared in *Rambler* 92, bring order out of chaos, and establish the truth of the matter:

> The task of criticism [is] to establish principles; to improve opinion into knowledge; and to distinguish those means of pleasing which depend upon known causes and rational deduction, from the nameless and inexplicable elegancies which appeal wholly to the fancy, from which we feel delight, but know not how they produce it, and which may well be termed the enchantresses of the soul. Criticism reduces those regions of literature under the dominion of science, which have hitherto known only the anarchy of ignorance, the caprices of fancy, and the tyranny of prescription. (*Works*, IV.122)

In these declarations of impersonal, impartial principle, there is a paradox for most readers of Johnson – and perhaps for Harold Bloom himself, who called Johnson the model of the 'strong' critic. There may be no quality of mind for which Johnson is better known than personal judgement. He exercised his judgement boldly in conversation and in writing, and he could be ruthlessly, even tyrannically, judgemental. We recall his verdict on Lady Diana Beauclerk, 'the woman's a whore, and there's an end on't' (*Life*, II.247); his interpretation of 'damned', 'Sent to Hell, Sir, and punished everlastingly' (*Life*, IV.299); his asides in the *Dictionary*, for instance when defining 'nowise': '*no* and *wise*: this is commonly spoken and written by ignorant barbarians, *noways*.' One key to understanding Johnson's literary criticism is to see how he reconciles his adherence to principles with his powerful personal judgement. He achieves this reconciliation in various ways at different times in his career, but there are common elements which unite his large body of critical writing.

To Err Is Human

Perhaps the most important assumption in Johnson's criticism is that writers are human beings performing a human task; they are fallible creatures like the rest of us, and their work is inevitably flawed. The most famous demonstration of this Johnsonian conviction is in his Preface to Shakespeare. After praising Shakespeare in the highest possible terms as 'the poet of nature', Johnson writes:

> Shakespeare with his excellencies has likewise faults, and faults sufficient to obscure and overwhelm any other merit. I shall shew them in the proportion in which they appear to me, without envious malignity or superstitious veneration. No question can be more innocently discussed than a dead poet's pretensions to renown; and little regard is due to that bigotry which sets candour [kindness] higher than truth.   (*Works*, VII.71)

All human worth is relative, as all human excellence is mixed with failure, and Shakespeare (whether we mean the writer or his works) is human. This may be hard to accept. Even now, in a post-Romantic era, Johnson's reference to Shakespeare as 'a dead poet' may strike some readers as disrespectful or even sacrilegious. It certainly would have sounded that way to Romantic critics such as Samuel Taylor Coleridge, who referred to Shakespeare as 'ever-living'.[2] But it is also a plain statement of fact.

Johnson takes the same realistic approach to every writer and to every work. After calling *Paradise Lost* first in design and second in performance 'among the productions of the human mind' (*Lives*, I.282), Johnson inevitably writes, 'The defects and faults of *Paradise Lost*, for faults and defects every work of man must have, it is the business of impartial criticism to discover' (I.288). This truth may not be universally acknowledged, but for Johnson it is indispensable.

Johnson applies the principle that writers are fallible human beings not only to the greatest authors but a fortiori to all those beneath them, and he did so at all stages of his career, often revealing interesting details in his view of authorial fallibility. In his review of the Duchess of Marlborough's memoirs (1742), for example, Johnson begins by pointing out the special access to truth obtained by those with first-hand knowledge of important public events and persons:

> The universal regard, which is paid by mankind to such accounts of publick transactions as have been written by those who were engaged in them, may be, with great probability ascribed to that ardent love of truth, which nature has kindled in the breast of man, and which remains even where every other laudable passion is extinguished. We cannot but read such narratives with uncommon curiosity, because we consider the writer as indubitably possessed of the ability to give us just representations.

However, the sentence continues, '[we] do not always reflect, that, very often, proportionate to the opportunities of knowing the truth, are the temptations to disguise it' (*Works*, XX.66–7).

To cite another early work, the *Life of Richard Savage* (1744), Johnson gives a typically mixed evaluation of his poetry. For instance, 'his diction is elevated, though sometimes forced, and his numbers sonorous and majestic, though frequently sluggish and encumbered. Of his style, the general fault is harshness, and its general excellence is dignity; of his sentiments, the prevailing beauty is sublimity, and uniformity the prevailing defect' (*Lives*, III.188). When Johnson wrote an abstract of Savage's life for the *Gentleman's Magazine* in 1753, he skipped some of the details of this evaluation and wrote simply, 'the versification and sentiments have a cast peculiar to themselves ... and, upon the whole, their beauties greatly exceeded their defects' (*Works*, XIX.254). He seems not merely to be expressing his opinion but to be weighing up a work with impartial scales.

With rare exceptions (perhaps only his early, eulogistic lives, such as the 'Life of Hermann Boerhaave'), Johnson takes this balancing-scales approach to every writer and to most of their works. It is most obvious in the *Lives of the Poets*, where Johnson is more overt about everything he believes, but it is always present.

Historical Context

Alongside the principle of human fallibility, Johnson recognizes that writers live in particular places at particular times; the critic, he believes, must keep that context in mind before passing judgement. Johnson's letter in 1754 to Thomas Warton in reaction to his recently published *Observations on the Faerie Queene of Spenser* provides the clearest expression of this Johnsonian critical principle. It has justly been cited as a founding document in historical criticism:

> You have shown to all who shall hereafter attempt the study of our ancient authours the way to success, by directing them to the perusal of the books which those authours had read. Of this method Hughes [an earlier editor of Spenser] and Men much greater than Hughes seem never to have thought. The Reason why the authours which are yet read of the sixteenth Century are so little understood is that they are read alone, and no help is borrowed from those who lived with them or before them. Some part of this ignorance I hope to remove by my book [the *Dictionary*] which now draws towards its end. (*Letters*, I.81)

The historical sense that Johnson thought necessary includes knowledge of linguistic development. His *Dictionary* is an historical record of English, like the *OED*, and a work that is sometimes called 'lower criticism' – that is, textual analysis of (usually ancient) works. Johnson was of course influenced by this humanist tradition of philological scholarship (see Chapter 4), but he also paid close attention to the social context of literary works. In his Preface to Shakespeare, for instance, having argued against the Aristotelian unities of time and place in drama, Johnson nevertheless offers an apology for Shakespeare's violations of them.

> Every man's performances, to be rightly estimated, must be compared with the state of the age in which he lived, and with his own particular opportunities; and though to the reader a book be not worse or better for the circumstances of the authour, yet as there is always a silent reference of human works to human abilities, and as the enquiry, how far man may extend his designs, or how high he may rate his native force, is of far greater dignity than in what rank we shall place any particular

> performance, curiosity is always busy to discover the instruments, as well as to survey the workmanship, to know how much is to be ascribed to original powers, and how much to casual and adventitious help. The palaces of Peru or Mexico were certainly mean and incommodious habitations, if compared to the houses of European monarchs; yet who could forbear to view them with astonishment, who remembered that they were built without the use of iron?
>   The English nation, in the time of Shakespeare, was yet struggling to emerge from barbarity. (*Works*, VII.81).

All human works are mixtures of success and failure, partly because they are products of their times.

Book History

Johnson was interested in what he called, and may have been the first to call, 'intellectual history' (*Works*, XVIII.98); he sometimes positioned quotations in his *Dictionary* to illustrate pieces of that history, and his preface to the Harleian Catalogue comprises one of the most important expressions of the idea. But he also knew that intellectual history was entangled with economic history, and his criticism is constantly aware of market forces, sales, publishing contracts, the vicissitudes of patronage, and the pressures of life in a garret. Books are not only made by writers; they also require publishers, printers, and distributors. In his 'Life of Pope', for instance, Johnson discusses sales of subscriptions for the *Iliad* translation. Everywhere, he shows a keen interest in contracts with booksellers. Boswell records moments of Johnson's conversation which displayed a similarly detailed fascination – for instance, his amused anger at the unjust contract foisted on Christopher Smart for the *Universal Visiter*:

> 'Old [Thomas] Gardener the bookseller employed [Richard] Rolt and [Christopher] Smart to write a monthly miscellany, called "The Universal Visitor" [sic]. There was a formal written contract, which Allen the printer saw ... They were bound to write nothing else; they were to have, I think, a third of the profits of this sixpenny pamphlet; and the contract was for ninety-nine years ... What an excellent instance ... of the oppression of booksellers towards poor authours!' (smiling) ...
> 'I wrote for some months in "The Universal Visitor", for poor Smart, while he was mad, not then knowing the terms on which he was engaged to write, and thinking I was doing him good. I hoped his wits would soon return to him. Mine returned to me, and I wrote in "The Universal

Visitor" no longer.' (*Life*, II.344–45; the contract is reprinted in *Bibliography*, I.664–9)

Johnson's interest in publishing history is partly personal. He grew up in the trade because his father was a bookseller, and when he went to London in 1737 it was to make his way in his father's industry. Johnson's awareness of the economics of publishing directly affects his process of critical evaluation: a writer's first responsibility, he realizes, is to be sure his books will be purchased and read. The 'Life of Pope' addresses one criticism of Pope's *Iliad* – that the translator added 'many *Ovidian* graces not exactly suitable to his [Homer's] character'. Here is Johnson's answer:

> To a thousand cavils one answer is sufficient; the purpose of a writer is to be read, and the criticism which would destroy the power of pleasing must be blown aside. Pope wrote for his own age and his own nation: he knew that it was necessary to colour the images and point the sentiments of his author; he therefore made him graceful, but lost him some of his sublimity. (*Lives*, IV.74)

This principle is perhaps the most durable article of faith in all of Johnson's criticism. It is found as late as the 'Life of Pope' (1781) and as early as the 'Life of Hermann Boerhaave' (1739), who 'knew that but a small part of mankind will sacrifice their pleasure to their improvement; and those authors who would find many readers, must endeavour to please while they instruct' (*Works*, XIX.51–2).

The obligation upon writers to reach their intended readership is a prevalent theme throughout the *Rambler*. It is built into the relationship between Mr Rambler and his audience, which Johnson is at pains to develop from the very first number (see Chapter 2). In *Rambler* 23, he deliberates over whether he should follow his own lights or tread the paths illuminated by the expectations of his readers. Finally, he decides that 'he who endeavours to gain many readers, must try various arts of invitation, essay every avenue of pleasure, and make frequent changes in his methods of approach' (*Works*, III.129). In the Preface to Shakespeare, the theme reaches its finest expression: 'every man finds his mind more strongly seized by the tragedies of Shakespeare than of any other writer; others please us by particular speeches, but he always makes us anxious for the event, and has perhaps excelled all but Homer in securing the first purpose of a writer, by exciting restless and unquenchable curiosity, and compelling him that reads his work to read it through' (*Works*, VII.83).

This vein of thought runs especially strongly through the *Lives of the Poets*, nowhere more so than in the 'Life of Dryden', where Johnson waxes poetic on the theme:

> Works of imagination excel by their allurement and delight; by their power of attracting and detaining the attention. That book is good in vain, which the reader throws away. He only is the master, who keeps the mind in pleasing captivity; whose pages are perused with eagerness, and in hope of new pleasure are perused again; and whose conclusion is perceived with an eye of sorrow, such as the traveller casts upon departing day. (*Lives*, II.147)

Criticism Is Literature

The simile at the conclusion of that passage reminds us that, for Johnson, criticism was a genre of literature. Not only must criticism, like other literature, please; it must express the experience and sensibility of the critic, and if there is little response to express, that is in itself a form of critical condemnation. In his 'Life of Swift', Johnson indicates his disapprobation of Swift's poetry by refusing to discuss it for more than half a page. He begins with the definitive statement: 'In the Poetical Works of Dr. Swift there is not much upon which the critick can exercise his powers.' To analyse the poems would be, he concludes briskly, 'to find faults of which the author could not be ignorant, who certainly wrote often not to his judgment, but his humour' (*Lives*, III.214).

At other times, Johnson registers his pleasure and approbation by rising to metaphor. His criticism, in effect, weighs out his literary experience and values it in the coin of literary language. Appropriately, Shakespeare evokes the most richly metaphorical passages in Johnson's criticism:

> The sand heaped by one flood is scattered by another, but the rock always continues in its place. The stream of time, which is continually washing the dissoluble fabricks of other poets, passes without injury by the adamant of Shakespeare. ... His characters are praised as natural, though their sentiments are sometimes forced, and their actions improbable; as the earth upon the whole is spherical, though its surface is varied with protuberances and cavities. (*Works*, VII.70-1)

Lesser writers evoke less magnificent imagery even when they are praised. Abraham Cowley's poem *The Chronicle* is 'a composition unrivalled and alone: such gaiety of fancy, such facility of expression, such varied similitude, such a succession of images, and such a dance of words, it is vain to expect except from Cowley. His strength always appears in his agility; his volatility is not the flutter of a light, but the bound of an elastick mind' (*Lives*, I.215). The critical style expresses the reader's experience, and even imitates that experience: 'Expect' and its anagram 'except' come together here because Cowley and other 'metaphysical poets' (as Johnson dubbed them) are fond of word games.

No treatment of Johnson's use of metaphor in literary criticism would be complete without citation of his grand contrast between the prose of Pope and that of Dryden in the 'Life of Pope':

> Poetry was not the sole praise of either; for both excelled likewise in prose; but Pope did not borrow his prose from his predecessor. The style of Dryden is capricious and varied, that of Pope is cautious and uniform; Dryden obeys the motions of his own mind, Pope constrains his mind to his own rules of composition. Dryden is sometimes vehement and rapid; Pope is always smooth, uniform, and gentle. Dryden's page is a natural field, rising into inequalities, and diversified by the varied exuberance of abundant vegetation; Pope's is a velvet lawn, shaven by the scythe, and levelled by the roller.   (*Lives*, IV.65)

As the note in the Yale edition indicates (*Works*, XXIII.1190n1), Johnson used a similar metaphoric scheme in the Preface to Shakespeare fifteen years earlier:

> The work of a correct and regular writer is a garden accurately formed and diligently planted, varied with shades, and scented with flowers; the composition of Shakespeare is a forest, in which the oaks extend their branches, and pines tower in the air, interspersed sometimes with weeds and brambles, and sometimes giving shelter to myrtles and roses.   (*Works*, VII.84)

The correspondence here suggests that Johnson's critical metaphors are expressions of an underlying, stable view of literature. Like a scientific model, Johnson's approach organizes the perceptions and responses of the critic or investigator. This underlying model is dualistic: it balances key elements in traditional definitions of poetry, such as delight and instruction or unity and variety. These binaries provide the basic structure of Johnson's criticism. That the binaries are often expressed in terms of floral diversity or mineral hardness is a sign that Johnson intends his criticism to be as scientifically precise as natural philosophy; but what guarantees that precision is the fixed underlying pattern of Johnson's thought, to which we will now turn.

The General

For Aristotle, art is an imitation of nature – a view which has been mainstream almost ever since, notwithstanding Oscar Wilde's brilliant reversal of the formula. But what is nature? As Raymond Williams astutely observed in his seminal work *Keywords*, it is 'perhaps the most complex word in the language'.[3] Even if we narrow the question down to the use of 'nature' in literary-critical language, it remains highly complex. Johnson's deployment of the word goes a long way in defining his view of art and his assumptions as a critic.

In Johnson's criticism, the elevation of 'nature' is another way in which to remove criticism from opinion to science. In his most famous use of the term, he amplifies its meaning by attaching the word 'general'. He also refers to 'general passions and principles', a phrase which implicitly gestures towards a conception of human nature:

> Nothing can please many, and please long, but just representations of general nature. Particular manners can be known to few, and therefore few only can judge how nearly they are copied. The irregular combinations of fanciful invention may delight a-while, by that novelty of which the common satiety of life sends us all in quest; but the pleasures of sudden wonder are soon exhausted, and the mind can only repose on the stability of truth.
>
> Shakespeare is above all writers, at least above all modern writers, the poet of nature; the poet that holds up to his readers a faithful mirrour of manners and of life. His characters are not modified by the customs of particular places, unpractised by the rest of the world; by the peculiarities of studies or professions, which can operate but upon small numbers; or by the accidents of transient fashions or temporary opinions: they are the genuine progeny of common humanity, such as the world will always supply, and observation will always find. His persons act and speak by the influence of those general passions and principles by which all minds are agitated, and the whole system of life is continued in motion. (Preface to Shakespeare, *Works*, VII.61–2)

In 1773, when he revised the *Dictionary*, Johnson returned to this theme, quoting under the definition of 'nature' a passage from Joshua Reynolds's Discourse IV (1771). Given Johnson's reluctance to quote from living authors, he clearly thought it worth making an exception – and indeed this is the most recently published citation in the whole *Dictionary*:[4]

> The works, whether of poets, painters, moralists, or historians, which are built upon general *nature*, live for ever; while those which depend for their existence on particular customs and habits, a partial view of *nature*, or the fluctuation of fashion, can only be coeval with that which first raised them from obscurity. Present time and future may be considered as rivals, and he who solicits the one must expect to be discountenanced by the other.

As both the definition and Reynolds's phrasing imply, 'general nature' has an entirely different artistic quality from a 'partial view of nature'. Poetry, to maintain its equivalence with general nature, must be comprehensive.

Comprehensiveness comes up as a feature of poetry and poets most emphatically in *Rasselas*, when Imlac lists the qualifications necessary to be a poet. It is a long list:

> the knowledge of nature is only half the task of a poet; he must be acquainted likewise with all the modes of life. His character requires that he estimate the happiness and misery of every condition; observe the power of all the passions in all their combinations, and trace the changes of the human mind as they are modified by various institutions and accidental influences of climate or custom, from the spriteliness of infancy to the despondence of decrepitude. He must divest himself of the prejudices of his age or country; he must consider right and wrong in their abstracted and invariable state; he must disregard present laws and opinions, and rise to general and transcendental truths, which will always be the same: he must therefore content himself with the slow progress of his name; contemn the applause of his own time, and commit his claims to the justice of posterity. He must write as the interpreter of nature, and the legislator of mankind, and consider himself as presiding over the thoughts and manners of future generations; as a being superiour to time and place.
> His labour is not yet at an end. (*Works*, XVI.44–5)

After hearing Imlac's speech, Rasselas says, 'Enough! Thou hast convinced me, that no human being can ever be a poet.' The impossible dream of the poet is, in sum, to understand general nature or, as Imlac puts it, to achieve a consciousness that is 'superior to time and place'.

Although real poets must live in particular times and places, they can approach the general in their writing. There is an important hint towards the achievement of the general earlier in Imlac's speech:

> 'The business of a poet', said Imlac, 'is to examine, not the individual, but the species; to remark general properties and large appearances: he does

not number the streaks of the tulip, or describe the different shades in the verdure of the forest. He is to exhibit in his portraits of nature such prominent and striking features, as recal the original to every mind; and must neglect the minuter discriminations, which one may have remarked, and another have neglected, for those characteristicks which are alike obvious to vigilance and carelesness.' (*Works*, XVI.43–4)

There is an assumption in Johnson's thinking of what A. O. Lovejoy, in his intellectual history of the eighteenth century, called 'uniformitarianism'.[5] This view sees an underlying skeleton of qualities in human beings, as well as in flora and fauna, that is the same at all times and places, despite differences in appearance, in dress, in political opinions, station in life, and so on. Literary works which reveal this underlying skeleton win Johnson's highest approval; those which do not are seen as failures.

So Johnson makes nature something eternal and unchanging. His 'general nature' has connections with broader movements in intellectual history, but it functions in his literary criticism mainly as a way of elevating his critical language and making it more scientific.

Because general nature and the representations of species rather than individuals are the aims of art, Homer is for Johnson the greatest writer of all time. William Windham reported him saying, 'The source of everything in or out of nature that can serve the purpose of poetry, [is] to be found in Homer; – every species of distress, every modification of heroic character, battles, storms, ghosts, incantations, &c.'[6] In *Rambler* 92, he calls him 'the father of all poetical beauty' (IV.123). Such comments echo Pope's famous remark in his *Essay on Criticism* that '*Nature* and *Homer* ... [are] ... the same' (l. 135). Next to Homer is Shakespeare, as the quotation on p. 86 makes clear.

On the other hand, Johnson is impatient with writers who do not capture general nature. The metaphysical poets, he argues, do not excel in poetry but only in wit ('Life of Cowley', *Lives*, I.200). Mark Akenside does not offer nature, and so nothing he does sticks with the reader:

> His images are displayed with such luxuriance of expression, that they are hidden, like Butler's Moon, by a *Veil of Light*; they are forms fantastically lost under superfluity of dress. . . . The words are multiplied till the sense is hardly perceived; attention deserts the mind, and settles in the ear. The reader wanders through the gay diffusion, sometimes amazed, and sometimes delighted; but, after many turnings in the flowery labyrinth, comes out as he went in. He remarked little, and laid hold on nothing. ('Life of Akenside', *Lives*, IV.173)

The Common Reader

'Nature' is not the only crucial term in Johnson's critical vocabulary. Another is 'truth' – as demonstrated in the passage quoted on p. 86 from the Preface to Shakespeare, where Johnson writes: 'the mind can only repose on the stability of truth' (*Works*, VII.62). Somewhere in the background is Christ's statement in the Gospels that 'I am the way, the truth and the life', although, as we point out in concluding this chapter, Johnson is quite clear about the superiority of religion to literature of any kind.

Another crucial word, is 'reader'. True, from one perspective readers are merely members of an unruly mob whose judgements are unstable and worthless. As Johnson says in *Rambler* 2, when he is still self-consciously sketching the relationship between Mr Rambler and his audience:

> He that endeavours after fame by writing, solicits the regard of a multitude fluctuating in pleasures, or immersed in business, without time for intellectual amusements; he appeals to judges prepossessed by passions, or corrupted by prejudices, which preclude their approbation of any new performance. Some are too indolent to read any thing, till its reputation is established; others too envious to promote that fame, which gives them pain by its increase. What is new is opposed, because most are unwilling to be taught; and what is known is rejected, because it is not sufficiently considered, that men more frequently require to be reminded than informed. The learned are afraid to declare their opinion early, lest they should put their reputation in hazard; the ignorant always imagine themselves giving some proof of delicacy, when they refuse to be pleased: and he that finds his way to reputation, through all these obstructions, must acknowledge that he is indebted to other causes besides his industry, his learning, or his wit.   (*Works*, III.14)

Here, as elsewhere in Johnson's work, the author's task seems hopeless. Yet at other times, the reader is exalted into the opposite type: a kind of ideal reader denoted by the general term 'the public'. *Rambler* 23 even asserts that 'the publick, which is never corrupted, nor often deceived, is to pass the last sentence upon literary claims' (*Works*, III.128).

Even though it is exalted in this passage and others, the 'public' usually retains an element of instability. In *Adventurer* 138, yet another of Johnson's many essays on the plight of poets, he writes that 'If mankind were left to judge for themselves, it is reasonable to imagine, that of such writings, at least, as describe the human passions, and of which every man carries the archetype within him, a just opinion would be formed.' But of course they are not left to themselves; they are misled by critics who are 'lazy', 'timorous', and more inclined to censure than to praise (*Works*, II.496).

In the Preface to Shakespeare, and elsewhere in his criticism, Johnson introduces an important qualification: the mere 'public' becomes the near-infallible 'mankind' through the passage of time:

> to works not raised upon principles demonstrative and scientifick, but appealing wholly to observation and experience, no other test can be applied than length of duration and continuance of esteem. What mankind have long possessed they have often examined and compared, and if they persist to value the possession, it is because frequent comparisons have confirmed opinion in its favour . . . what has been longest known has been most considered, and what is most considered is best understood. (*Works*, VII.59–61)

Late in life, when Johnson wrote the *Lives of the Poets*, he shifted the terminology from 'mankind' to 'the common reader'. The two are not precisely equivalent of course, but they both represent idealized forms of public opinion.

Johnson's most famous invocation of the phrase 'the common reader' – the one that Virginia Woolf adopted as the title of her collected works of criticism – occurs in the 'Life of Gray', in an evaluation of the *Elegy Written in a Country Churchyard* (1751). The evaluation appears out of sequence, since it was not Gray's last work: his Pindaric odes (1757) and his translations from Norse (1761) were later. As Roger Lonsdale points out in his edition of the *Lives*, Johnson 'held back his eloquent tribute to the *Elegy Written in a Country Churchyard* . . . in the belief that it would conclude not merely "Gray" itself, but his entire survey of English poetry. "Lyttelton" in fact replaced "Gray" at the end of the rearranged *Lives* (1781)' (*Lives*, IV.500), but Johnson did not know this would happen at the time that he wrote his famous final evaluation. Johnson fashioned his praise of the *Elegy* in contrast to his criticism of the obscurity and self-consciously learned style of Gray's odes; but more significantly, it was designed as Johnson's final statement of literary-critical principle:

> In the character of his Elegy I rejoice to concur with the common reader; for by the common sense of readers uncorrupted with literary prejudices, after all the refinements of subtilty and the dogmatism of learning, must be finally decided all claim to poetical honours. The *Church-yard* abounds with images which find a mirrour in every mind, and with sentiments to which every bosom returns an echo. (*Lives*, IV.184)

Lawrence Lipking has written eloquently on this passage (as Lonsdale notes), praising it at different times either as Johnson's resignation of critical authority, or as an attempt to merge his views with those of a broader public.[7] Both of Lipking's perceptions may be true, but it is also true that Johnson began creating this exalted 'common reader' much earlier, usually substituting the grander name of 'mankind', 'the public', or – in *Rambler* 52 – the 'common voice of the multitude' (*Works*, III.280). The familiarity of the term 'common reader', by contrast, its lack of grandeur, signifies a kind of polite condescension. But like all of Johnson's terms, it reconciles for a moment the science of criticism with the impartial, inevitable, and natural test of time.

Beyond Criticism: Religion and the Sublime

If critics must yield to time and the common reader, they must also give way before the demands of religion. Criticism is in Johnson's view, quoted at the beginning of this chapter, 'only to be ranked among the subordinate and instrumental arts'. In the ranking in *Rambler* 208, in which criticism comes in third, 'The essays professedly serious' come in first. On the basis of these essays, Mr Rambler hopes he 'can be numbered among the writers who have given ardour to virtue, and confidence to truth' (*Works*, V.320).

Johnson's belief that criticism is subordinate and instrumental to religion and morality has ramifications throughout his criticism. In a more explicit way than other religious critics (C. S. Lewis, say, or Northrop Frye), Johnson makes religion and morality part of the evaluative calculus. In his evaluation of Shakespeare, for example, after praising him to the skies, he says, 'His first defect is that to which may be imputed most of the evil in books or in men. He sacrifices virtue to convenience, and is so much more careful to please than to instruct, that he seems to write without any moral purpose' (*Works*, VII.71). (The notion of morality without religion was a fringe view in Johnson's day, and certainly not one he held.) Johnson goes so far as to suggest emendations to the text of Shakespeare that would improve their moral quality. His suggestion of 'world' for 'word' in Macbeth's speech on learning of the death of his wife (see p. 72 above) is a good example. So is Johnson's related tendency to explicate Shakespeare's 'hidden' moral judgements throughout his plays (see pp. 75–6). This is one way that criticism yields to religion in Johnson's evaluations of literature.

Another, interesting effect of religion on Johnson's criticism is his denigration of religious poetry. In the 'Life of Waller', Johnson pauses to explain his views on this subject:

> Let no pious ear be offended if I advance, in opposition to many authorities, that poetical devotion cannot often please. . . . Contemplative piety, or the intercourse between God and the human soul, cannot be poetical. Man admitted to implore the mercy of his Creator, and plead the merits of his Redeemer, is already in a higher state than poetry can confer. The essence of poetry is invention; such invention as, by producing something unexpected, surprises and delights. The topicks of devotion are few, and being few are universally known; but, few as they are, they can be made no more; they can receive no grace from novelty of sentiment, and very little from novelty of expression. . . .
> The ideas of Christian Theology are too simple for eloquence, too sacred for fiction, and too majestick for ornament. (*Lives*, II.52–3)

In the *Lives of the Poets* Johnson applies this principle to Waller's religious verse, to Cowley's *Davideis*, to Isaac Watts's devotional poetry, and even to Pope's *Messiah*, which he himself translated into Latin. The real test of its durability as a critical principle for Johnson is, however, in its potential application to Milton's *Paradise Lost*. With the possible exception of Shakespeare, Milton provides the most interesting subject of Johnson's criticism. Christine Rees in *Johnson's Milton* (2010) has documented and commented incisively on Johnson's almost lifelong engagement with Milton both as a poet and as a politician. For many readers in the eighteenth century, Milton was still remembered as a regicide at the same time that he was glorified as England's national poet. Johnson made many explicit and implicit judgements on Milton throughout his life. As a young man, he argued about his politics with Gilbert Walmesley and other Lichfield Whigs; in middle age, he became involved with one William Lauder, who blamed Milton for the downfall of the House of Stuart and, through forgery, sought to prove that Milton was a plagiarist. Johnson regretted his involvement when he realized Lauder was a forger, but he never gave in to critics who refused to believe anything negative about England's Homer. Attacked for doubting Milton's genius and originality, Johnson fought back in the *Rambler* by pointing out faults in Milton's prosody. The message there, as in so much of Johnson's criticism, is that Milton was only a man, and therefore subject to error.

In the *Lives of the Poets* Johnson had his final reckoning with Milton. Of course, he found faults in Milton's poetry, even in *Paradise Lost*, which obviously stands out as the greatest of Milton's works to Johnson and everyone else (see p. 80). His praise of *Paradise Lost*, however, is very grand; it excels in important ways even his praise of Shakespeare. Deliberating on *Paradise Lost*, Johnson goes back to basics: 'Poetry is the art of uniting pleasure with truth, by calling imagination to the help of reason. Epick poetry undertakes to teach the most important truths by the most pleasing precepts' (*Lives*, I.282). Outlining all the areas of knowledge an epic poet must master, in the manner of Imlac's impossible criteria for excellence in poetry in Chapter X of *Rasselas*, Johnson begins his analysis:

> Bossu is of opinion that the poet's first work is to find a *moral*, which his fable is afterwards to illustrate and establish. This seems to have been the process only of Milton; the moral of other poems is incidental and consequent; in Milton's only it is essential and intrinsick. His purpose was the most useful and the most arduous; *to vindicate the ways of God to man* [sic]; to shew the reasonableness of religion, and the necessity of obedience to the Divine Law. (*Lives*, I.283)

There can be no higher praise than this. His approach is a little oblique, and possibly a bit grudging, because he references a French critic, an upholder of neoclassical norms – the kind that he dismissed in his evaluation of Shakespeare. It should be remembered, however, that Johnson said it would have been better if Shakespeare had obeyed the French rules of the drama. Critically, they are right, even if 'there is always an appeal open from criticism to nature' (*Works*, VII.67). Here, in any event, Milton has obeyed the rules; in fact, he is unique in doing so, which may or may not be praise. But the important point is that his 'purpose is the most useful and the most arduous'.

The morality of *Paradise Lost* puts it above every other poem, but Johnson's praise of this key feature is somewhat understated. Criticism, like poetry, cannot add much to religious truth. Instead, Johnson expends his finest critical language on the purely literary aspects of Milton's poem: its characteristic sublimity and its 'gigantick loftiness'. He also brings the work back down to the human level: by pointing out its faults ('the want of human interest is always felt . . . None ever wished it longer than it is' (*Lives*, I.290); by tracing the history of its composition back to the Trinity College manuscripts, which suggest that Milton first planned it as a drama; and even by glancing at the neo-Latin poems from which Lauder claimed it was stolen. Romantic critics, such as Charles Lamb, did not even want to see the earlier drafts, preferring to imagine that the work sprang whole from Milton's mind in a kind of Athenian birth. This could never have been Johnson's ideal.

His first principle of criticism holds firm, then, even for the greatest of all poetical works, and even when that greatness is closely linked to religious truth. Books are written by human beings, not gods: they are therefore faulty, and they arise out of particular life experiences in particular places and particular times. Criticism, as a formal art with its own, often French, rules can offer a framework for analysis, but critics are also human and can only report on their own experience of literature. They must do this even though, at the same time, they must be aware of things beyond their individual experience: formal critical rules and, most important of all, the purifying effect of time – which will eventually pass a permanent judgement on all works of literature, including any critic's own.

Figure 6.1 *Walking up the High Street* by Thomas Rowlandson.
Courtesy of the Lewis Walpole Library, Yale University.

Chapter 6

Social and Political Thinker

> *The great benefit of society is that the weak are protected against the strong. The great evil of confusion is that the world is thrown into the hands, not of the best, but of the strongest.*
> (Sermon 23, *Works*, XIV.246)

Johnson's politics are something of a puzzle. By selecting the evidence carefully, one could easily construct two opposing portraits of him. The first portrait would show a forward-thinking political moderate, driven above all by compassion: far ahead of his time on penal reform, unequivocally opposed to slavery, sceptical about Britain's expanding empire and the wars fought for it. He could be scathing about kings and prime ministers alike and is a noted figure in the history of press freedom; he could identify the middle ground, once arguing that 'A wise Tory and a wise Whig, I believe, will agree' (*Life*, IV.117); he consistently sympathized with the underdog, drew attention to the cruelties of British society, and declared that 'a decent provision for the poor, is the true test of civilization' (*Life*, II.130).

The other portrait – probably the dominant one in Johnson's lifetime and for nearly 200 years after – would begin from Johnson's self-identification as a Tory and note his *Dictionary* definition of the word: 'One who adheres to the antient constitution of the state, and the apostolical hierarchy of the church of England'. In 1783, a year before his death, Johnson looked back ruefully at the previous twenty years and consoled himself that 'I have at least endeavoured to preserve order and support Monarchy' (*Letters*, IV.124). This was the Johnson who felt 'The crown has not power enough' (*Life*, II.170), scorned all demands for American independence, and opposed the entrance to English universities of those who deviated from the Anglican Thirty-Nine Articles. It was also – there is no ignoring it – the Johnson given to remarks such as 'I am willing to love all mankind, *except an American*' (*Life*, III.290) and 'The first Whig was the Devil' (*Life*, III.326).

How to combine these two portraits? Though chronology is highly important, the difficulty cannot simply be explained by saying that there was an early, rebellious Johnson, and a later, conservative one. And a further complication is that Johnson could make strongly apolitical statements: 'I would not give half a guinea to live under one form of government rather than another. It is of no moment to the happiness of an individual', he told Adam Ferguson in 1772 (*Life*, II.170). There is a hint of self-description in Johnson's comment on Lyttelton: 'Politicks did not, however, so much engage him as to withhold his thoughts from things of more importance' (*Lives*, IV.186).

Johnson's politics take their inspiration from those 'things of more importance'. When he spoke on the controversies of his day, as he frequently did, his views were informed by deeper and more general principles.

The Individual and Society

'The business of life', Johnson writes, 'is carried on by a general co-operation' (*Adventurer* 137, *Works*, II.489); it is up to each person to play their part by helping others to live:

> The apparent insufficiency of every individual to his own happiness or safety, compels us to seek from one another assistance and support. The necessity of joint efforts for the execution of any great or extensive design, the variety of powers disseminated in the species, and the proportion between the defects and excellencies of different persons, demand an interchange of help, and communication of intelligence, and by frequent reciprocations of beneficence unite mankind in society and friendship.   (*Rambler* 104, *Works*, IV.190)

In this great system, everyone has their role to play: 'Providence always gives us something to do' (*Letters*, II.313). As that phrase suggests, Johnson's view of society is profoundly Christian. Whatever our social position or line of work, we are to rely on the 'care of Providence' (*Adventurer* 107, *Works*, II.445), to remember that everyone will be judged at the end of time, and to find peace in trusting that God will reward all good efforts, even if they seem to fail. For Johnson, it is Christianity which most effectively upholds the 'great law of mutual benevolence' (*Rambler* 183, *Works*, V.197).

Our mutual need of each other should bring us together. We are social animals; hence Johnson's love of conversation, 'the most eligible amusement of a rational being' (*Rambler* 89, *Works*, IV.108) and his conviction that 'Life has no pleasure higher or nobler than that of friendship' (*Idler* 23, *Works*, II.72). He thought the human invention which had produced most happiness was 'a good tavern or inn' (*Life*, II.452). But this sociability means that we want both to help each other and hurt each other. 'From that social desire of being valuable to each other, which produces kindness . . . it proceeds, and must proceed, that there is some value in being [able] to give pain' (*Letters*, I.304).

Central to Johnson's thought is his awareness of the Christian doctrine of original sin – each person's strong, irrational tendency towards evil. We are caught in between kindness and cruelty, 'attracted towards each other by general sympathy, but kept back from contact by private interests' (*Adventurer* 45, *Works*, II.360). Earthly contentment depends above all on individuals choosing to treat each other with love and kindness, rather than envy and malice: 'To receive and to communicate assistance, constitutes the happiness of human life' (*Adventurer* 67, II.389). Johnson sees a role for the state in helping to preserve these benign relationships: as he writes in *Idler* 22, 'The end of all civil regulations is to secure private happiness from private malignity' (*Works*, II.70). This *Idler* laments the current state of debtors' prisons, in which the penniless were put at the mercy of their creditors. It is, Johnson writes, a much-abused and unjust system: he proposes new regulations to give the creditors less power.

However, politics can also drive people apart. Much as Johnson admired his friend Edmund Burke, he took a dim view of Burke's close adherence to the Rockingham Whigs. Not only did political parties discourage independent thought, they also played into the conflicts of society. The 'rage of party' made people hate anybody 'whose education or reflections, have inclined him to sentiments, different from their own' (Sermon 27, *Works*, XIV.296).

In 1770, Johnson lamented that 'The papers of every day have been filled with the exhortations and menaces of faction' (*Works*, X.324). 'Faction' is a frequent term of disapproval. Johnson could himself be virulently factional in his dislike of Whigs; but he felt that political partisanship, as well as obscuring the complexity of political questions, broke up the human community.

Compassion

A theistic worldview such as Johnson's risks complacency. If society is overseen by God, one way of thinking goes, then perhaps some people are simply meant to be oppressed and downtrodden – it is all part of the divine plan. The belief in Providence becomes an excuse for cruel inequalities. To be fair to Johnson, he was well aware of this possible conclusion. And he loathed it, as we know from one of his best-known performances, the review of Soame Jenyns's *A Free Inquiry into the Nature and Origin of Evil* (1757). If a thinker is revealed by what makes them angry, then few texts are so important in understanding Johnson as this denunciation of social indifference. Normally, he tempered his anger or channelled it into irony. Here, he is uncompromising.

Johnson does try to avoid personal hostility, by praising some of Jenyns's book; but when Jenyns casually remarks that being poor has its consolations, such as having 'a more exquisite relish of the smallest enjoyments' (*Works*, XVII.405), Johnson says straightforwardly that Jenyns does not know what he is talking about. Those who argue for the happiness of poverty 'perhaps never saw the miseries which they imagine thus easy to be born' (XVII.407). Then Jenyns speculates that earthly unhappiness might be justified because it entertains some unknown race of superior creatures, who are experimenting on us for their delight. Cue several paragraphs of Johnson's most devastating satirical writing:

> Many of the books which now croud the world, may be justly suspected to be written for the sake of some invisible order of beings, for surely they are of no use to any of the corporeal inhabitants of the world. Of the productions of the last bounteous year, how many can be said to serve any purpose of use or pleasure. The only end of writing is to enable the readers better to enjoy life, or better to endure it: and how will either of those be put more in our power by him who tells us, that we are puppets, of which some creature not much wiser than ourselves manages the wires. (*Works*, XVII.421)

It was Jenyns's nonchalant treatment of human 'miseries' that was so infuriating. For Johnson, 'there is scarcely any virtue, that we ought more diligently to exercise than that of compassion to the needy and distressed' (Sermon 4, *Works*, XIV.39). His life expressed the point more clearly than anything he wrote. Hester Thrale Piozzi said she had never known anyone who loved the poor so much, and reckoned that he had given away the vast majority of his income. Nor was Johnson judgemental towards the recipients. After he gave a half-crown to a poor woman who appeared shortly afterwards in fine new clothes, Johnson shrugged: 'if it gave the woman pleasure, why should she not wear them?' (*Miscellanies*, II.416). As his letters show, he was constantly raising money for good causes and hatching schemes to help young acquaintances find work and education. He chose to share his home with a group of difficult and rather desperate characters (see Chapter 1).

The countless examples of Johnson's kindness give weight to his insistence on 'that habitual sympathy and tenderness, which, in a world of so much misery, is necessary to the ready discharge of our most important duties' (*Rambler* 80, *Works*, IV.57). Nor should kindness be limited to personal action; Johnson raised several protests against institutional cruelty and injustice. If his awareness of 'a world of so much misery' can lend a daunting grimness to his writing, it also activates his compassion. *Rambler*s 170–1, for instance, tell a harrowing story of a woman's descent into prostitution, showing her as the victim of wicked exploitation.

Johnson's views on capital punishment distinguished him from his contemporaries. *Rambler* 114 protests against the use of the death penalty for minor crimes such as theft. This essay came not long after Henry Fielding's influential 1751 tract suggesting that the laws were lax enough already and that the real need was for stronger policing – an argument which reflected conventional wisdom and was welcomed by a House of Commons committee on the issue.[1]

Civilization and Order

Next to the pretty Minster Pool in Lichfield, a three-minute walk from the house where Johnson spent most of his first twenty-five years, there is a small plaque above a doorway. It marks the spot where Lord Brooke, the Parliamentarian general, was killed in 1643 during the first siege of Lichfield Cathedral. Within living memory, just about, Johnson's hometown had been a war zone. And he described the Civil War in horrified tones: 'Our laws were over-ruled, our rights were abolished. The soldier seized upon the property, the fanatick rushed into the church' (Sermon 23, *Works*, XIV.247). War was the ultimate breaking of ties – the dissolving of social bonds into a violent power struggle.

In one sense, Johnson suggested, civil unrest should be expected: 'all rebellion was natural to man' (*Life*, V.394). The articulate and clever, then, can make a name for themselves by posing as revolutionaries: 'He that contradicts acknowledged truth will always have an audience; he that vilifies established authority will always find abettors' (*Thoughts on Falkland's Islands* [1771], *Works*, X.376). Johnson regarded with contempt those intellectuals, like John Knox and John Milton, who used their gifts in the service of revolution.

Johnson valued hierarchy – 'subordination' – because it stood against social breakdown and allowed people at every level of society to flourish. As the historian John Cannon has written, 'subordination' meant to Johnson 'not humiliation or degradation, but order, harmony, stability, and security'.[2] A stratified society was a sign of progress: Johnson, unlike Rousseau, thought mankind had benefited from increasing sophistication.

For Johnson, the alternative to hierarchy – given humanity's tendency towards malicious competition – was not a happily egalitarian world, but 'a perpetual struggle for precedence' (*Life*, I.448). The monarchy, for instance, is supposed to signify (he wrote as early as 1738) 'conservation of our religious and civil rights, and protection from slavery and arbitrary power' ('Pamphilus on Condolence', *Works*, X.10). When Johnson's *Political Tracts* were published in 1776, he added a quotation from Claudian to the title page which translates as: 'Whoever thinks it slavery to be under an outstanding monarch is mistaken; no more delightful liberty exists than under a virtuous king' (*Works*, X.313n3). Johnson also believed that 'There is a reciprocal pleasure in governing and being governed' (1763; *Life*, I.408), though he knew well that those who command are often inhumane to those who obey. He would have agreed with Simone Weil, who wrote that 'Obedience being a necessary food of the soul, whoever is definitely deprived of it is ill'.[3]

All that having been said, Johnson wrote and spoke dismissively of several individual kings; even when he praises George III, he immediately contrasts him with his second-rate predecessors (*The False Alarm*, *Works*, X.342). Some of Johnson's bolder statements have been taken as evidence that he was a Jacobite, angling for the return of the Stuarts to the British throne. This question has provoked an extensive and impressively bad-tempered scholarly debate. Certainly, Johnson saw the Jacobite claim very clearly and could sympathize with the cause strongly; but he described the actual Jacobite uprising of 1745 as 'contemptible' and expressed relief that 'through the favour of providence' it 'was crushed at once' (*Works*, XX.224).

Here, as elsewhere, Johnson prioritized order and peace. He wanted to protect the political system which had emerged over time, with its balance of monarchy, aristocracy, and commons. He saw the present state of affairs as a hard-won historical achievement threatened by subversion at home and abroad.

Since the divisions of the Civil War had a significant religious element, Johnson emphasized the need for Christian unity. His attachment to the established Church of England was partly based on his own piety: as Boswell noted, religion was 'the predominant object of his thoughts' (*Life*, I.69), and Johnson was a man of frequent prayer who considered his first duty was to love and serve God. Moreover, he thought religion brought the best out of the human race: 'Christianity is the highest perfection of humanity' (*Letters*, I.269). Less idealistically, Johnson's Anglicanism was a matter of political order. Religious difference is so explosive a threat to a society that, even if a ruler was 'morally or theologically wrong' in his beliefs, he would still be 'politically right' to restrain other beliefs: 'no member of a society has a right to *teach* any doctrine contrary to what that society holds to be true' (*Life*, II.249). Despite this, Johnson worried that 'If nothing may be published but what civil authority shall have previously approved, power must always be the standard of truth' ('Life of Milton', *Lives*, I.252). And he did not want a theocracy – from his early translation of Lobo's *Voyage to Abyssinia* onwards, he denounced the coercion of religious belief as unChristian.[4] Still, he felt the state should take strong measures – such as the exclusion from Oxford and Cambridge of everyone except orthodox Anglicans – to keep a single belief system in place.

The fear of violent social breakdown should be kept in mind when approaching Johnson's views on political order, which are otherwise easily framed as the diatribes of an insecure authoritarian. Certainly, there is something distasteful about several of Johnson's statements on 'the rabble'. But these were volatile times: during the Wilkite crisis, mobs marched through Johnson's part of London, smashing the windows of their opponents; the anti-Catholic Gordon Riots of 1780 left (to quote William Cowper) 'a Metropolis in flames and a Nation in Ruins';[5] and in the seventy-five years after Johnson's death, almost every major European state would be convulsed by revolution. Tensions were sufficiently high in January 1783 for Johnson to write to John Taylor: 'I am afraid of a civil war' (*Letters*, IV.109).

Despite his preference for subordination, Johnson favoured social mobility (see pp. 110–12, on Scotland), and *Rambler* 57 suggests that, with a sharing of resources, there could be 'an universal exemption from want' (*Works*, III.307). Unlike more reactionary commentators, he was pleased by advances in industry and technology which allowed a new, moneyed class to challenge the interests of the aristocracy. But he accepted the basic stratification of society with the monarchy at the top, then the aristocracy, then the rest. Those who challenged this order – the Whigs – he saw as the greatest enemies of the poor and vulnerable. 'Severity towards the poor' was 'an undoubted and constant attendant or consequence upon whiggism' (*Miscellanies*, I.204).

Johnson was no sentimentalist about the monarchy and aristocracy. He was no snob, either. If he doubted egalitarian democracy, it was from a double fear: first, of the intolerant violence of mass popular movements; and secondly, of a callous world of dog-eat-dog competition in which the weakest are forgotten.

In 1881, Leslie Stephen called Johnson 'the embodiment of sturdy prejudice, or staunch beliefs which had survived their logical justification ... the last of the Tories'.[6] Scholars have demolished that kind of misrepresentation by showing the flexibility and depth of Johnson's thought. If he criticized his age for its perceived obsession with the new, he also celebrated modern trends, such as scientific and commercial progress, a better-educated and better-read public, and the increasingly humane treatment of the vulnerable.

A recent historian of the Enlightenment drags up the old misrepresentation, introducing 'the cantankerous, obese, arch-conservative Samuel Johnson'.[7] But one does not normally find cantankerous arch-conservatives of any body type making this kind of prediction:

> There is reason to expect, that as the world is more enlightened, policy and morality will at last be reconciled, and that nations will learn not to do what they would not suffer. (*Thoughts on Falkland's Islands, Works*, X.354)

No question has been more heatedly contested in the last thirty years of Johnson studies than the exact nature of his politics. If Johnson was no 'staunch', 'sturdy' 'arch-conservative', how should we describe him? As a Tory, even a Jacobite? A humanitarian pragmatist? A moderate of no definite allegiance, but unusual eloquence and moral seriousness? It may be helpful, in getting a handle on Johnson's social and political thought, to introduce a distinction which Christopher Ricks has made with reference to Johnson's literary criticism. Johnson, Ricks writes, preferred principles to theory: having established the principles of a particular matter, he chose 'to think thereafter about the application of the principles rather than to elaborate principle into theory'.[8] Johnson's basic principles – about the way society works, the duty of compassion, the need for order – emerged over time.

The Opposition Journalist

Johnson's first political writings, from 1738 onwards, are those of an eager young polemicist who believes he has identified the real enemies of the common good: in this case, the government led by the de facto prime minister Robert Walpole. The opposition to Walpole was politically diverse, but Johnson was closest to the 'Patriot' group, itself a broad church. In these early writings, Johnson accuses Walpole's administration of incompetence and a cowardly foreign policy, but also immorality and hostility to religion (*A Compleat Vindication of the Licensers of the Stage, Works*, X.70, 66) and a lack of intellectual and literary sophistication (65–6). Walpole and his men were selfish, corrupt, and uninterested in the verdict of posterity, which would no doubt condemn them. *London* (1738) lumps together political tyranny, corruption in high places, humiliation on the international stage, French cultural influence, immorality, and injustice in one general denunciation of the state of things.

Above all, Johnson saw Walpole's government as threatening individual liberties. A piece attributed to him refers to the 'duty to warn a people against any intended encroachments upon their rights or liberties' ('To Mr Urban', *Works*, XX. 35). Among the encroachments against which Johnson warned are the existence of a standing army, which seemed ready for use against the people; alleged state manipulation of the law courts; and censorship, the target of Johnson's satirical *Compleat Vindication of the Licensers of the Stage* (1739). The licensers in question – the Lord Chamberlain and his assistants, all of them Walpoleans – had suppressed a play, Henry Brooke's *Gustavus Vasa*, which told of a corrupt prime minister being overthrown along with the foreign king who had backed him. The *Compleat Vindication* impersonates a government stooge who demands submission to 'authority' and is outraged at the 'irreverence' of the government's critics.

Another perceived crime of Walpole's government was its attempt to stop the reporting of debates in the Commons. The *Gentleman's Magazine* came up with a solution: to have an insider pass on notes of the debates and then write up thinly disguised versions of what had been said. It fell to Johnson to do the writing, and so he spent the early 1740s immersed in the minutiae of political debates (see Chapter 2). Perhaps this experience played a part in the cooling off of his political zeal. Certainly, when Walpole did fall, disillusion soon set in. The leaders of the 'Patriot' opposition, with which Johnson had broadly aligned himself, accepted positions of power and, as Johnson saw it, sold out on their principles: this is one source of his 1775 quip, 'Patriotism is the last refuge of scoundrels', which Boswell silently altered to 'a scoundrel' (*Life*, II.348).

Perhaps the early Johnson's tone was more urgent than his real feelings. Years after, he rather came round to Walpole, seeing him as a decisive leader of a kind Britain needed in the crises of the 1770s. Johnson remained sensitive to the cause of civil liberties, saying that *habeas corpus*, the right not to be arbitrarily imprisoned, was 'the single advantage which our government has over that of other countries' (*Life*, II.73); but he became less passionate about the freedom of the press, reasoning that the press itself could be manipulated by the government.[9] What remained part of Johnson's thought, more than his specific positions, is a strong moral sense, and an impatience with sloppy thinking and irresponsible language.

The next twenty years saw Johnson busy with the *Dictionary* and the *Rambler*, as well as innumerable smaller pieces of writing, not much of it directly political. But there were some memorable exceptions. During the Seven Years' War, a huge success for Britain's imperial expansion,

Johnson was a sceptical observer, though not exactly a pacifist. At a time of nationalistic fervour, he described the Franco-British conflict over America as a morally bankrupt exercise in shameless exploitation:

> the French and English quarrelled about the boundaries of their settlements, about grounds and rivers to which, I am afraid, neither can shew any other right than that of power, and which neither can occupy but by usurpation, and the dispossession of the natural lords and original inhabitants. Such is the contest that no honest man can heartily wish success to either party ... The American dispute between the French and us is therefore only the quarrel of two robbers for the spoils of a passenger. (*Observations on the Present State of Affairs*, *Works*, X.186–8)

Johnson's writing often tends towards blunt realism – even when he is writing on matters of political theory. Take his anonymous collaboration with Robert Chambers, Oxford's Vinerian Professor of Law, on a series of lectures (1767–73) which dealt with the foundations of society. Though Johnson's exact contribution is unknown, it seems to have been substantial, and some of his political principles were firmed up by the work. One central theme of the lectures is that society's foundation lies, not in an original social contract, but in the sheer collective need for some absolute authority.[10]

In 1762, Johnson took a decision which would bring him back into the heart of the political debate: he accepted a pension from the government. The political situation had changed greatly since the days of Walpole; the new King, George III, wanted to unify the different political groupings, and Johnson was one of many formerly dissenting voices who now came within the fold of the establishment. His pension was meant as a recognition of a major writer; but it also made Johnson a closer ally of the government, and it was natural that he would enter into controversy on its behalf.

The Pamphleteer

To his critics, Johnson was the government's bootlicker, defending the ministry in return for his pension. But his four pamphlets of the 1770s are unquestionably honest; he sincerely believed that 'the crown has not power enough', and that at a time of rising instability, there were serious threats from political radicalism and American revolution. Three of his pamphlets respond to specific crises: *The False Alarm* (1770) on the issue of John Wilkes, *Thoughts on Falkland's Islands* (1771) on a territorial dispute with Spain, and *Taxation No Tyranny* (1775) on America. One common feature of these three pamphlets is their analytical detail; another is Johnson's suspicion of his opponents' motives.

The False Alarm deals with the crisis over Wilkes, the exhibitionist MP for Middlesex whom the House of Commons had expelled on the grounds that he had been convicted of libel and obscenity. Wilkes continued to contest his seat from prison; he won three more times, and each time the Commons refused to admit him, finally handing the Middlesex seat to a candidate with a comparatively tiny share of the vote. Many saw this as endangering the British constitution itself. The expression 'alarming crisis' became a catchphrase in political debate, and Johnson's pamphlet kicks it around: 'this alarming crisis . . . such an *alarming crisis* . . . we hear of nothing but of an alarming crisis of violated rights' (*Works*, X.332–5). It is all an artificial fuss, says Johnson. 'Nothing, therefore, is necessary, at this *alarming crisis*, but to consider the alarm as false' (X.345).

False because the Wilkites' legal arguments are full of holes, he says, discussing a variety of complex parliamentary precedents. But even if they had a point, it is hardly a cause for such melodramatic rhetoric. The whole case has been blown out of proportion. When the country had been passionately divided before, it had at least been over something that mattered:

> The civil war was fought for what each army called and believed the best religion, and the best government. The struggle in the reign of Anne, was to exclude or restore an exiled king. We are now disputing, with almost equal animosity, whether Middlesex shall be represented or not by a criminal from a jail. (*Works*, X.343)

The whole kerfuffle, in other words, is a national embarrassment. And the guilty parties are those who have dressed up their own political interests as a great struggle for 'liberty', trying to destabilize the government for the sake of personal ambition. Most of them 'may justly be suspected of not believing their own position' (X.324) – they simply want to 'oppose the ministry' and are prepared to use 'Every artifice of sedition' (324); as a result, 'so much violence of discontent has been excited' (333). But their arguments, *The False Alarm* suggests after 'punctiliously and minutely' examining them, do not add up to much (332). The petitions raised around the country are evidence, not of genuine public anger, but of the conformism and vague-minded excitement which local activists have managed to stimulate. Petitions were being signed by thousands who did not 'know, till they are told, that any privilege had suffered violation' (339); 'Those who are sober enough to write add their names, and the rest would sign it if they could' (337).

Johnson comments witheringly: 'how near must be the ruin of a nation that can be incited against its governors, by sophistry like this' (330). The inciters are stupid, but more importantly, irresponsible: do they know the terrible energies they are trying to stir up? The shadow of civil war falls across this piece, as with so much of Johnson's political writing.

Thoughts on Falkland's Islands summarizes in depth the history of these territories – their discovery, the competing claims of Spain and Britain over them – and the recent crisis, in which a Spanish general called Madariaga seized the islands. The government had negotiated a deal whereby the islands would be restored to Britain, and the question of who owned them was temporarily placed on the back burner.

'Moderation' is Johnson's keyword – the virtue exercised by the government (*Works*, X.365, 381) and also by Madariaga (X.361). As a result of this moderation, Britain has regained the islands, while allowing the larger question of sovereignty to remain in the balance. Given the complex history of the region, Johnson argues, it is fatuous to reproach the government for not demanding that Spain accept British sovereignty: 'To push advantages too far is neither generous nor just' (368). The avoidance of war is not a sign of the government's weakness, but of its wisdom: 'they were able to obtain by quiet negotiation all the real good that victory could have brought us' (372). Violent nationalism, 'the military ardour of the publick' (374), produces 'that wantonness of bloodshed that has so often desolated the world' (372); Johnson looks back to the casualty-heavy battle for Havana in the Seven Years' War and shudders: 'May my country be never cursed with such another conquest!' (374). Only 'vultures waiting for a day of carnage' – that is, opposition figures who hoped to make political capital from an unsuccessful war – could be disappointed at the avoidance of war (384).

America became a major issue in these years, as the colonists grew restive against British supremacy. In *The Patriot*, Johnson had summed up the situation by arguing that Britain had a natural and lawful authority over its own colonies: after all, they were established 'by an English charter; and have been defended by English arms' (*Works*, X.397). For the colonists to imagine that, having grown prosperous thanks to British help, they could suddenly claim autonomy, was 'an accumulation of absurdity'. The British claim was simply one of justice. 'We have always protected the Americans; we may therefore subject them to government' (397).

In *Taxation No Tyranny*, Johnson repeats those points and scrutinizes the colonists' arguments. For instance, they assert that, since they could not vote, they should be exempt from governmental commands. However, Johnson points out, many Britons cannot vote, and even of those who do, a sizeable majority do not get the representatives they voted for. Johnson proposes that a massive military force be sent, in the hope that the Americans would back down without a fight and so 'this commotion may end without bloodshed' (*Works*, X.452).

Taxation No Tyranny is one of Johnson's less distinguished pieces – not so much for its content as for its style, mainly dry and, when it strikes a more polemical note, hardly vintage Johnson. The exception is a gibe which has gone down in history, aimed at the slave owners who complained about British tyranny: 'how is it that we hear the loudest yelps for liberty among the drivers of negroes?' (*Works*, X.454).

Once more, Johnson singles out opportunistic British politicians as 'Those who most deserve our resentment' (X.452). The Americans have been 'encouraged and incited by ... men whom they thought their friends, but who were friends only to themselves'. As in *The False Alarm*, Johnson identifies the irresponsibility of the politically ambitious as the root cause of the crisis.

Each of these pamphlets applies cool analysis to what Johnson thought a dangerously inflamed public debate. This brings us to another common feature of the pamphlets – and probably the most disconcerting for the modern reader – namely, Johnson's apprehensions about democracy. In *The Patriot* (written in time for the 1774 general election), Johnson warns:

> Few errors, and few faults of government can justify an appeal to the rabble; who ought not to judge of what they cannot understand, and whose opinions are not propagated by reason, but caught by contagion.   (*Works*, X.391)

It is worth saying that Johnson did once refer to himself as a member of 'the rabble' (*Life*, II.153), and he favoured some kinds of democratization. *The Patriot* congratulates the parliament which passed the 1770 Elections Act, removing Parliament's privilege of deciding electoral disputes in the constituencies: 'They ... shewed that they were more willing than their predecessors to stand on a level with their fellow-subjects' (*Works*, X.398). But he still felt that those in power should protect the people 'not only from being hurt by others, but from hurting themselves' (X.395). The 'rabble' were being used by political opportunists – a dominant theme of these pamphlets, and especially of *The Patriot*. Like *The False Alarm* and *Taxation No Tyranny*, its title is meant to undermine the language of Johnson's opponents. Claiming to be a 'patriot' had become a cliché, and Johnson, with his limited faith in mankind's natural goodness, riffs on the unscrupulousness of the self-styled lovers of their country. Some are genuine; but

> the greater, far the greater number of those who rave and rail, and enquire, and accuse, neither suspect, nor fear, nor care for the public; but hope to force their way to riches by virulence and invective, and are vehement and clamorous, only that they may be sooner hired to be silent. (*Works*, X.391)

The Patriot attacks at length the self-interest of those who 'instigate the populace with rage' (391). 'He is no lover of his country, that unnecessarily disturbs its peace.' And Johnson returns to a matter dealt with in the *Thoughts on Falkland's Islands*. The clamour to wage war for the islands, when there was no military need, would have sacrificed human lives for political advantage:

> those who are now courting the favour of the people by noisy professions of public spirit, would, while they were counting the profits of their artifice, have enjoyed the patriotic pleasure of hearing sometimes, that thousands had been slaughtered in a battle, and sometimes that a navy had been dispeopled by poisoned air and corrupted food. (*Works*, X.396)

Such is the distance between party-political gamesmanship and the realities of human suffering.

A Journey to the Western Islands of Scotland

In 1773, Johnson and Boswell travelled around the Scottish Highlands. Both wrote accounts of it; while Boswell's is anecdotal and entertaining, Johnson's serves as his fullest depiction of a single society. The book illustrates his conviction that the 'general prosperity' of a nation should be estimated not in the lives of the elite, but 'in the streets, and the villages, in the shops and farms'; and still more specifically, in the small humdrum details of ordinary life (*Journey*, 16–17). So Johnson reports on the minute architectural features of people's houses, the local climate, the state of agriculture, what wildlife each area supports. Typical of his worldview is his comparison of Skye – where everyday products have to be bought from 'some wandering pedlar' – to Coll, which has an actual shop:

> To a man that ranges the streets of *London*, where he is tempted to contrive wants for the pleasure of supplying them, a shop affords no image worthy of attention; but in an Island, it turns the balance of existence between good and evil. To live in perpetual want of little things, is a state not indeed of torture, but of constant vexation. I have in *Sky* had some difficulty to find ink for a letter; and if a woman breaks her needle, the work is at a stop. (*Journey*, 108)

For all its attention to 'little things', the *Journey* is also a panoramic study of a culture undergoing a momentous transformation. The old Highlands was a feudal society in which the chieftains had hereditary powers to tax their subordinates, decide legal disputes, and wage battles against other clans. That old way of life, as Johnson noted, had already disappeared. The British government, in the wake of the Jacobite uprising, had removed much of the chieftains' legal authority and had struck at Highlander identity by banning traditional dress and the bearing of arms. Meanwhile, as the economy modernized, the chieftains had begun to raise rents, and tens of thousands of Scots were migrating to the American colonies, enticed by stories of a more prosperous life.

On Skye especially, Johnson surveys this period of transition and gives a balanced account of it. Modernization has had its drawbacks, Johnson suggests. A culture has almost vanished, and there were certain benefits to the old hierarchies: the tacksman, for instance, a middleman between landowner and tenant, could pass on useful knowledge. The landowners have become more profit-hungry, and this is helping to drive emigration – though Johnson suspects the migrants' dreams of fortune will prove illusory.

At the same time, Johnson hardly regrets the passing of feudalism. It was hostile to social mobility: 'Where there is no commerce nor manufacture, he that is born poor can scarcely become rich' (70). And those living for existence from day to day scarcely have time for far-sighted scientific and commercial enterprise. Feudalism had kept most Highlanders unfulfilled, impoverished, and without those benefits of civilization which Johnson praises wherever he finds them: law and order, scientific and industrial advance, 'elegance and culture' (21).

Still, Johnson wishes to celebrate what remains of benevolent authority: he praises, for instance, the Laird of Muck, who is 'very attentive' to the 'happiness' of his people and has provided them with the smallpox inoculation (57). And Johnson finished the book with another case of individual charity: an Edinburgh school for the deaf and dumb. 'It was pleasing to see one of the most desperate of human calamities capable of so much help' (136–7).

The concluding remark is characteristic of Johnson's emphasis on the role of moral goodness in the life of a society. 'No people', Johnson believed, 'can be great who have ceased to be virtuous' (*Works*, X.150). Ultimately, Johnson thought there was far more to life than politics. To Robert Chambers, with whom he had worked so closely in developing his political thought, he wrote in 1783:

> The state of the Publick, and the operations of government have little influence upon the private happiness of private men, nor can I pretend that much of the national calamities is felt by me. (*Letters*, IV.124)

Nothing, for Johnson, can shift the burden of personal responsibility. It is up to the individual to live a good life, follow their conscience, and fulfil their duties, and no government can do that for them. Moreover, everyday suffering from poverty and cruelty, though government can palliate it, also demands a more general responsibility: that of 'the great law of mutual benevolence' (*Works*, V.197). Johnson told Boswell once that 'politics go but a little way with me in comparison of religion'.[11] Since 'Christianity is the highest perfection of humanity', it holds out a hope which politics cannot match.

In lines contributed to Goldsmith's *The Traveller*, Johnson made a memorable statement of the limits of political action:

> How small, of all that human hearts endure,
> That part which laws or kings can cause or cure.   (ll. 429–30)

Politics could not fully confront the urgent questions of the human heart about how to live and what choices to make. But one activity which could confront such questions was literature; above all, perhaps, the literature of life-writing.

Figure 7.1 Johnson in 1775 by Sir Joshua Reynolds. © Courtesy of the Huntington Art Museum, San Marino, California.

Chapter 7

Biographer

> We are all prompted by the same motives, all deceived by the same fallacies, all animated by hope, obstructed by danger, entangled by desire, and seduced by pleasure.
> (*Rambler* 60, *Works*, III.320)

To devote an entire chapter of this book to a single genre might seem to require some justification. The justification is simply that, for Johnson, biography was the kind of literature he found most important and enjoyable. In conversation, he referred to 'the biographical part of literature, which is what I love most' (*Life*, I.425). According to *Rambler* 60, 'no species of writing seems more worthy of cultivation than biography, since none can be more delightful or more useful' (*Works*, III.319). The delightfulness is a matter of taste; the usefulness of biography, on the other hand, rests on Johnson's understanding of psychology, morality, literary theory, and anthropology.

Psychology because, in Johnson's view, human motivation is highly imitative. He mistrusted realistic novels, for instance, because they placed bad examples before the reader. Since 'the power of example is so great, as to take possession of the memory by a kind of violence', fiction could make us love charmingly wicked characters, to the point where their wickedness corrupts our own characters: 'as we accompany them through their adventures with delight, and are led by degrees to interest ourselves in their favour, we lose the abhorrence of their faults' (*Rambler* 4, *Works*, III.22–3). But by the same token, for Johnson, reading can also raise an audience's moral aspirations – the highest goal a writer can aim for.

Johnson preferred biography to fiction because biography presents the everyday, the normal and universal. Even lives which seem remarkable, he argues in *Rambler* 60 (his most significant treatment of the genre), are stories of vice and virtue, of dilemmas in how to live, which affect us all: 'there is such an uniformity in the state of man' that, in theory, a biography of *anybody* could be helpful and entertaining (*Works*, III.320). In biography, we are not merely lectured about the evils of greed or the importance of helping the poor – we see somebody else doing it and can imagine ourselves in their shoes, for good or ill.

What should a biographer do, then, if confronted with a less-than-perfect life? Here, Johnson's apparently ironclad theory of biography turns out to be more flexible. Once, as Boswell recorded, he claimed that it was better to pass over faults in silence – a biographer of the poet Parnell, for instance, shouldn't mention that he drank too much, in case the reader concluded that such behaviour was reasonable (*Life*, III.155). On an earlier occasion, however, Johnson had suggested that 'it would produce an instructive caution to avoid drinking, when it was seen, that even the learning and genius of Parnell could be debased by it' (III.155). Again, Johnson argued that a biography should mention its subject's weaknesses, since 'If nothing but the bright side of characters should be shewn, we should sit down in despondency, and think it utterly impossible to imitate them in *any thing*' (*Life*, IV.53). The biographer's task is always to tell an entertaining and morally improving story, but the means of doing so are complex and shifting. And while Johnson's approach to the genre changed over time, his goal remained the same.

Early Biographies

Johnson's major biographical works are the *Life of Savage* (1744) and the *Lives of the Poets* (1779–81), but even in his minor works one can discern his characteristic approach. The 'Life of Boerhaave', for instance, published in 1739, largely relies on a previous biography of the physician by Albert Schultens. Yet Johnson's departures from his source demonstrate his priorities clearly. For instance, to avoid driving the reader to despondency, he omits Schultens's treacly description of Boerhaave's marriage ('The sweet harmony of wills ... with which this most excellent couple passed *twenty-eight years*, cannot be expressed. The earth never produced a better husband').[1] It was the kind of unrealistic panegyric which was no use to anybody, because so far exalted beyond ordinary experience.

Johnson might also have thought it was untrue. For another of his preoccupations, visible throughout his career as a biographer, is a scepticism towards stories which are too neat, or for which the evidence is lacking. When Schultens praises Boerhaave's preternatural gifts for diagnosing illness, Johnson is more reticent: he has no way of telling, he says, which of the stories about Boerhaave's diagnostic insight are accurate, and which are legends (*Works*, XIX.21).

Above all, the early biographies are concerned with biography's great task of moral education. Religious piety takes first place as the virtue Johnson wishes to recommend to his reader. The 'Life of Browne' (1756) quite explicitly declares that, since people often reject or accept Christian belief 'upon the authority of those whom they think wiser than themselves', it is important to establish that a distinguished thinker like Browne was indeed a serious Christian believer (*Works*, XIX.340-1). At other times, he points us towards useful lessons in our own struggles with virtue and vice.

The 'Life of Confucius' again follows very closely an earlier biography, making Johnson's additions all the more telling. The earlier biographer, for instance, recorded that Confucius, when in the service of the King of Lu, had kept his head even when surrounded by the beautiful women at court. When the king and his other advisers had lost their way in partying with these 'alluring' creatures, Confucius wisely steered clear of all distractions and continued to focus on political matters (*Works*, XIX.225). First, Johnson draws an admiring conclusion: Confucius was not just a gifted philosopher, but someone who could live philosophically in the real world. 'It is no small addition to the honour of Confucius, that he remained uninfected amidst so fatal a contagion; a contagion against which the preservatives of philosophy have been often found of very little effect' (XIX.225). And that is not the end of the lesson: virtue, Johnson wants us to see, is not only a matter of solemn renunciation, but of gaining the strength to live well in the world. So later, when Confucius is reduced to humiliating poverty and is living on rice and water, he responds with great dignity and cheerfully accepts his situation; and Johnson emphasizes that this is only what one would expect, given the philosopher's previous self-restraint in the midst of temptation: 'how easily may he support pain, who has been able to resist pleasure' (XIX.226).

Characteristically, Johnson also draws the reader towards lessons about everyday behaviour, as opposed to dramatic moral struggles. His portrait of the clergyman Zachariah Mudge (1769) praises Mudge's 'firm and unshaken' belief, but what Johnson underlines is that Mudge was also gracious towards others – 'for knowing with how much difficulty truth was sometimes found, he did not wonder that many missed it' (*Works*, XIX.478). And while Mudge exhibited 'grandeur and solemnity' in the pulpit, when he sat down with his friends 'he was a companion communicative and attentive, of unaffected manners, of manly chearfulness, willing to please, and easy to be pleased' (XIX.479).

So consistent over time was Johnson's moral outlook that one can easily draw connections between his passing remarks in the early biographies and similar comments made decades after in the *Lives of the Poets*. In the 'Life of Milton', one of his last significant works, Johnson criticized insubordination and rebelliousness; in his life of the Parliamentarian churchman Francis Cheynell (1751), Johnson describes Cheynell as 'turbulent, obstinate and petulant' (*Works*, XIX.272): as well as lacking reverence towards his superiors at Merton College, Oxford, he spoke to them without 'modesty'. Once more, Johnson moves between a grand moral principle and a more everyday virtue.

Likewise, one of Johnson's most frequently repeated pieces of practical wisdom was the importance of bold determination over timidity. *Idler* 57, for instance, portrays the unfortunate Sophron, whose watchword is to 'run no hazards' and who therefore lives a dull life: 'Thus Sophron creeps along, neither loved nor hated, neither favoured nor opposed; he has never attempted to grow rich for fear of growing poor, and has raised no friends for fear of making enemies' (*Works*, II.178–80). The *Lives of the Poets* draws on this principle; the 'Life of Pope', for instance, affirms that 'Self-confidence is the first requisite to great undertakings' (*Lives*, IV.3). That principle is laid down as early in Johnson's career as his biography of the sea-captain Sir Francis Drake (1740–1). 'Resolution and success reciprocally produce each other', Johnson states (*Works*, XIX.108). The enemies of such resolution, however, make arguments against the success of any new undertaking and pour scorn on any original effort:

> there are some men of narrow views, and grovelling conceptions, who, without the instigation of personal malice, treat every new attempt as wild and chimerical, and look upon every endeavour to depart from the beaten track, as the rash effort of a warm imagination, or the glittering speculation of an exalted mind, that may please and dazzle for a time, but can produce no real or lasting advantage ... their notions and discourse are so agreeable to the lazy, the envious, and the timorous, that they seldom fail of becoming popular, and directing the opinions of mankind.   (XIX.126–7)

At the same time, Johnson writes, it is not enough to plan a great project, unless one has developed the habit of hard, careful work. The 'example of Drake' shows 'that diligence in employments of less consequence is the most successful introduction to greater enterprizes' (XIX.95). The same lesson is drawn in Johnson's biography of the scholar Jean-Philippe Baratier – whose brief life has 'given a proof of how much may be performed in so short a time by indefatigable diligence' (191) – and of Thomas Sydenham, where Johnson drives the lesson home with force: in a world of quackery and overconfidence, 'those who shall hereafter assume the important province of superintending the health of others, may learn from this great master of the art, that the only means of arriving at eminence and success are labour and study' (238).

In *Rasselas*, Johnson's Imlac tells the Prince, 'Few things are impossible to diligence and skill' (*Works*, XVI.56). When he came to write the *Lives of the Poets*, Johnson implied the same point, but less stridently, and sometimes by understatement: 'diligence is never wholly lost' ('Life of Collins', *Lives*, IV.121). Perhaps he had mellowed in his old age; perhaps those earlier exhortations were delivered partly to himself.

Biography at First Hand

The preceding section may make Johnson sound almost programmatic in his treatment of biography, as though he conceived of his task as the mining of individual lives for sermon material. His biographies of Richard Savage, his close friend, and Edward Cave, his one-time boss, are more tender, personal, and – in the case of Savage – internally conflicted about the different responsibilities of a friend and a biographer.

They also raise a question on which Johnson was certainly inconsistent. Is it necessary for a biographer to have first-hand knowledge of his subject? Johnson once told Boswell that 'They only who live with a man can write his life with any genuine exactness and discrimination' (*Life*, II.446), and he sometimes speaks and writes disparagingly of biographies which rely merely on previous written texts. A biography, after all, should deal with the great questions of right and wrong, happiness and unhappiness; these things are revealed more by the details of someone's everyday life than by their public achievements. '[B]iography has often been allotted to writers who seem very little acquainted with the nature of their task ... more knowledge may be gained of a man's real character, by a short conversation with one of his servants, than from a formal and studied narrative, begun with his pedigree, and ended with his funeral' (*Rambler* 60, III.322). Gossip and anecdote, not a recitation of achievements, were the crucial raw material of biography.

Yet this was more of an ideal Johnson hoped to achieve than a standard he rigorously adhered to. As Roger Lonsdale has pointed out, such remarks were made in the aftermath of the *Life of Savage* (1744), a biography of a close friend, and long pre-dated the *Lives of the Poets*, written with nothing like the same intimate knowledge of its subject. Although Johnson thought Goldsmith's *Life of Parnell* inadequate, his own biography of Parnell had to rely on it.[2]

The 'Life of Cave' (1754) demonstrates how Johnson put first-hand knowledge into effect. Cave's 'chilness', a steadiness of demeanour and a certain reserve, is presented as the key to his character. 'His mental faculties were slow. He saw little at a time, but that little he saw with great exactness ... His affections were not easily gained, and his opinion not quickly discovered' (*Works*, XIX.300–1). Cave might seem not to be listening, while actually taking a close interest and forming plans around what you were telling him. To friends and enemies, he sometimes appeared disengaged – but would turn out to be unshakably loyal (and a man not worth crossing). All of this could only be gleaned from close personal acquaintance, and Johnson notes that only those who knew Cave (such as, by implication, the biographer) really grasped his character: 'His resolution and perseverance were very uncommon ... his constancy was calm, and, to those who did not know him, appeared faint and languid, but he always went forward though he moved slowly' (XIX.300). Once again, 'resolution and perseverance' are high on Johnson's list of practical virtues. Then, as a sign of his knowledge of Cave and a discreet gesture of posthumous affection, Johnson comments that one of the 'last acts of reason which he exerted, was fondly to press the hand which is now writing this little narrative' (see p. 25 above).

In writing Cave's life, then, Johnson drew on what he had seen with his own eyes, without disguising his affection for his subject. When, in 1743, he wrote *An Account of the Life of Richard Savage*, he had been able to do the same, but with a much more challenging subject. Savage was scarcely a model for the ordinary reader to follow: a bohemian poet who lived chaotically, spent money he didn't have, narrowly escaped the death penalty after being convicted of murder, and died probably on account of a lifetime's hard drinking. He therefore tests the Johnsonian theory of biography's usefulness and reveals its many dimensions.

Here Johnson had to face the question of judgement: how should such a life, in the end, be described? Should the decisive note be of praise or blame? In a sense, he dodges the question, writing in the penultimate paragraph that, given the immense disadvantages against which Savage had to struggle, people should be careful about drawing any conclusions: 'Those are no proper judges of his conduct, who have slumbered away their time on the down of plenty; nor will any wise man presume to say, "Had I been in Savage's condition, I should have lived or written better than Savage"' (*Life of Savage, Lives*, III.188). This point is anticipated very early in the *Life of Savage*, with the remark that Savage deserves 'a degree of compassion, not always due to the unhappy' (*Lives*, III.120). Johnson wants to remind the reader that judging is not a coldly intellectual matter; it is also a matter of the heart, of compassion. Later on, when Savage – in financial distress – produces a substandard work, it 'must rather excite pity than provoke censure' (III.130). When Johnson discusses Savage's ingratitude to his wealthy benefactors, he argues that since the benefactors were not especially harmed by this, such behaviour 'ought rather to have been pitied than resented; at least, the resentment it might provoke ought to have been generous and manly'

(177). In all of this, Johnson refuses to rest in judgement, to allow moral disapproval to have the stage to itself. He brings the reader face to face with Savage; at one point, as in the life of Cave, we are taken into an emotional scene between biographer and subject. Savage 'parted from the author of this narrative with tears in his eyes' (175). This comes after a passage which seems to satirize Savage's irresponsibility: it jolts us into a realization that Savage was a flesh-and-blood figure, not a mere example in a moral story.

At other times, without directly addressing the reader, Johnson seems to be gesturing towards the same point. 'Compassion was indeed the distinguishing quality of Savage', he writes of Savage's kindness towards a woman whose perjury at the murder trial nearly resulted in his own execution (*Lives*, III.138). Can the reader, he asks implicitly, show the same generosity? Johnson also makes compassion into a guiding principle beyond Savage's own life. When Savage and Richard Steele have a falling-out – Savage had mocked Steele behind his back, so Steele withdrew his financial support – Johnson says that Savage shouldn't be blamed, because people often ridicule their acquaintances, and it shouldn't be taken as an exceptionally malicious act. But at the same time 'Sir Richard must likewise be acquitted of severity', since it was understandable for him to take offence (III.127). The tendency of the *Life of Savage* is towards acquittal, not a guilty verdict.

Again, Johnson appeals to the complexity of human motivation and character, to dissuade us from easy judgements. Perhaps Savage's 'misfortunes', he suggests, were in no small part due to Steele's 'example' of financial irresponsibility (III.126). This point, too, Johnson makes indirectly as well as directly: in a description of Savage's mind, he notes the poet's understanding of 'the innumerable mixtures of vice and virtue' which make up humankind (140). He quotes at length Savage's pious sentiments about trusting God even amid suffering (180).

All this, however, is only one half of the story. Johnson is prepared to blame Savage, showing how his impulsiveness, his willingness to take stupid risks and pursue immediate pleasures, alienated his friends and wrecked his prospects. Johnson sums it up like this: 'an irregular and dissipated manner of life had made him the slave of every passion that happened to be excited by the presence of its object, and that slavery to his passions reciprocally produced a life irregular and dissipated' (*Lives*, III.186). As Johnson narrates Savage's decline and fall, we become aware of an invisible character in the story: 'mankind'. Johnson observes, for instance, that although Savage was sometimes ill-treated by his friends, he was also a hard man to support: any money given to him would be spent immediately, and to invite Savage into one's home was to invite a complete overturning of domestic order and peace. 'It must therefore be acknowledged', Johnson writes, 'in justification of mankind, that it was not always by the negligence or coldness of his friends that Savage was distressed' (III.166–7). The *Life* is not just about one person, but about how his story relates to our universal human nature.

Johnson approvingly notes that Savage himself took a fundamentally positive view of mankind: 'I can produce the suffrage of Savage in favour of human nature' (III.186). Yet, by the same token, Savage should be judged by the standards mankind holds in common. Just as Johnson wished to agree with the 'common reader' about poetry (see Chapter 5), so he thought that the general social consensus should be given a privileged place. For instance, Johnson frowns on Savage's habit of befriending people and then publishing mordant satires of them. There might be some principled reasons for acting like this, Johnson observes, but such reasons 'are very seldom satisfactory to mankind' (141). The common opinion of the average man or woman has an authority of its own.

And this, in the end, tilts the balance of the *Life of Savage* back towards condemnation rather than sympathy. Johnson will make some allowances for Savage; but in the end, Savage's flagrant contradiction of ordinary moral standards cannot be allowed to pass. In a resounding final paragraph – which Johnson added on second thoughts[3] – he holds up Savage as an example of someone who contradicts 'common' wisdom: 'those, who, in confidence of superior capacities or attainments, disregard the common maxims of life, shall be reminded, that nothing will supply the want of prudence; and that negligence and irregularity, long continued, will make knowledge useless, wit ridiculous, and genius contemptible' (*Lives*, III.188). This is a leading principle of Johnson's literary biographies: that those who are 'superior' in their intellectual or artistic abilities may also be decidedly inferior in other respects. The *Life of Savage* pays tribute to how Savage used his literary abilities: 'These writings may improve mankind, when his failings shall be forgotten.' But the biographer, since he preserves those failings for posterity, is also obliged to make some comment on them.

The Lives of the Poets

Never again, after the *Life of Savage*, would Johnson write so focused and dramatic a portrait of a single life. But the questions which animated the *Life of Savage* are everywhere in his last major work, the *Lives of the Poets*. Not that the *Lives* is an especially coherent work, in its planning or execution. It was, in the first place, not actually Johnson's idea. Rather, it originated in a rivalry between different publishers. In 1777, a group of leading London booksellers decided to crush a competitor's series of the works of English poets by producing their own series – one which would outdo its competitor in illustrations, quality of paper, and, crucially, in a celebrity endorsement. The collections would each bear a short introduction by Samuel Johnson.

From the beginning, then, Johnson was playing catch-up to someone else's project; he claimed, for instance, that he only recommended five poets for the series, the other forty-seven being the publishers' choice – and he makes some half-suppressed grumbles about this division of responsibility.[4] The 'Life of Milton' begins with the weary remark that he doesn't have much to add to the work of previous biographers; it's merely that 'a new narrative was thought necessary to the uniformity of this edition' (*Lives*, I.242). Yet the subsequent narrative is one of Johnson's most celebrated and characteristic works. It is also far longer than the short introductions which Johnson originally agreed to provide; between 1777 and the spring of 1778, the project had become a much bigger one in Johnson's mind, to the extent that the *Prefaces* ended up being published separately, rather than as curtain-raisers to the poets' works. As a result, the publishers got a bargain: having been contracted to write some brief pieces, Johnson wrote at whatever length he felt like – and discovered that, after a lifetime of reading and thinking about these poets, he had a great deal to say. By March 1781, when the final volumes were published, he had created a monumental work.

Monumental but also whimsical: Johnson covers what he wants to cover, until exhaustion or a lack of interest overcomes him. The 'Life of Dryden' is thorough in places, but he openly admits that he wishes he didn't have to revisit Dryden's entire dramatic oeuvre (*Lives*, II.81), and twice says it would be too 'tedious' to go into detail about all Dryden's minor works (98, 102).

The research-heavy aspect of writing biography did not come naturally to Johnson. As Roger Lonsdale observes, 'Knowledgeable early reviewers and readers often noted the absence of new information in the first *Prefaces*, precise and detailed as they may now appear to be' (*Lives*, I.88). He started diligently, writing letters in search of fresh information and visiting the Bodleian Library in Oxford; he got some research help from the printer John Nichols and a couple of other literary friends; but this conscientious beginning did not last, and much of the *Lives* simply relied on previous accounts.[5]

It is ironic, then, that Johnson would so often lament the inadequacy of these earlier biographers. In 1773, he had said in conversation that 'he did not think that the life of any literary man in England had been well written' (*Life*, V.240), and the *Lives* often tut-tut at previous attempts. The 'Life of Smith' actually quotes a previous biography at full length, then gleefully punctures it by pointing out that the authors were hopelessly biased. The 'Life of Cowley' opens with a breezy condemnation of 'the penury of English biography', including Thomas Sprat's biography of Cowley (*Lives*, I.191). But at the end, Johnson actually recommends the Sprat version. The biographer's task turned out to be more arduous than Johnson might have suspected.

That said, Johnson was aware that literary biography often suffered from a lack of source material. 'It often happens to writers', he had remarked in the 'Life of Roger Ascham' (1762), 'that they are known only by their works; the incidents of a literary life are seldom observed, and therefore seldom recounted' (*Works*, XIX.427). The 'Life of Dryden' expresses disappointment at the lack of relevant anecdotes. What had made the *Life of Savage* so vivid – Johnson's first-hand knowledge of his subject – could not be replicated elsewhere.

Truth and Justice

Yet even when a biographer has no special extra knowledge to offer, there are other ways to correct the record. Throughout the *Lives*, Johnson casts doubt on stories, not because he has discovered some new documentary evidence, but because – by implication – he is a man of the world who knows how the record gets distorted. A story of Milton's turning down a job offer arouses Johnson's scepticism: 'large offers and sturdy rejections are among the most common topicks of falsehood' (*Lives*, I.264). When Waller is supposed to have uttered a brilliant one-liner to King James II, Johnson wonders whether it was really him: 'Pointed axioms, and acute replies, fly loose about the world, and are assigned successively to those whom it may be the fashion to celebrate' (*Lives*, II.42). Another genre of false anecdote is the tale of so-and-so being offended by such-and-such – as with the story that Addison was stung by Pope's political statements in *Windsor Forest*. 'Reports like this are often spread with boldness very disproportionate to their evidence' ('Life of Pope', *Lives*, IV.11). At other times, Johnson's advance on other biographers is that he presents differing theories without deciding between them. How was Waller's Royalist plot discovered? '[T]he question cannot be decided' (*Lives*, II.35).

There is a more exalted sense, too, in which the biographer can exert judgement on existing material. The *Lives* self-consciously aim to correct the record for the sake of justice. For instance, if major writers deserve a biographical tribute, so do the teachers who made them what they were, and Johnson is constantly at pains to detail his subjects' years of schooling: 'Not to name the school or the masters of men illustrious for literature, is a kind of historical fraud, by which honest fame is injuriously diminished: I would therefore trace him through the whole process of his education' ('Life of Addison', *Lives*, III.1).

The same principle had appeared much earlier, in the *Life of Savage*, where Johnson praised one of Savage's relatives who stuck with him despite his reputation – a woman 'whose name I am now unable to recollect, and to whom therefore I cannot pay the praises which she deserves' (*Lives*, III.129). A biographer is a kind of dispenser of praise and honour, who should take care to give it to the right people. In the 'Life of Watts', Johnson says that Thomas Abney's kindness to Watts 'deserves a particular memorial' (IV.106).

But it is for the poets themselves that Johnson reserves the highest honours. For if, as the Preface to the *Dictionary* asserted, 'The chief glory of every people arises from its authours' (*Works*, XVIII.109), then authors must be given their special podium in the national hall of fame. When Dryden published his *Aeneid*, 'the nation considered its honour as interested in the event' (*Lives*, II.144*)*. Denham was 'a genius born to improve the literature of his country' (I.235). Butler's life is shrouded in uncertainty, but his 'name can only perish with the language' (II.4). The *Lives* accepts its duty in defining the canon and giving due respect to literary greatness.

At the same time, Johnson does not let us forget that such greatness counts for less, ultimately, than moral goodness. The 'Life of Watts' is merely polite about Watts's writing but awestruck by the man's virtues; the 'Life of Milton', as we will see, is spectacularly irreverent despite Johnson's lavish praise for *Paradise Lost*. Characteristically, when Johnson discusses Cowley's self-censorship to avoid political persecution, he writes: 'let neither our reverence for a genius, nor our pity for a sufferer, dispose us to forget that, if his activity was virtue, his retreat was cowardice' (*Lives*, I.195). Genius is not a get-out-of-jail-free card.

Lives and Works

Almost all of the *Lives* are divided into two: first the biography, then some literary-critical remarks (covered in Chapter 5). A few *Lives* – Milton, Waller, Dryden, Addison, Swift, Pope – also include a central section on the subject's character. The structure was not Johnson's invention, and it is in some ways artificial since life and work intersect throughout. Sometimes they are kept carefully apart. Congreve is praised for his literary skill in comedies whose moral implications Johnson later condemns; Otway's *The Orphan* demonstrates both the author's personal weaknesses and his perceptiveness as an observer. The 'Life of Pope' repeatedly warns the reader not to be charmed by Pope's skill into accepting his faulty philosophy. These warnings are gentler in the biographical section; only in the second half does Johnson bluntly write that 'Never were penury of knowledge and vulgarity of sentiment so happily disguised' as in the *Essay on Criticism* (*Lives*, IV.76).

Yet a man and a poet are one person, not two; and Johnson is prepared to judge both at once. Waller's poetry, because it demonstrates his political two-facedness, is evidence of 'a prostituted mind' (II.40). Is that the biographer speaking, or the literary critic? It is both, since they are both studying one mind. The 'Life of Dryden' is an extended case study in the same principle. Although Johnson refers to the sentimentalism of *All for Love* as 'rather moral than critical' (*Lives*, II.96), the two categories are not hermetically sealed. Dryden's works are what they are, with their strengths and weaknesses, because he had 'a mind better formed to reason than to feel' (II.134). More critically, Johnson finds in one of Dryden's dedications (to Mary of Modena) 'a strain of flattery which disgraces genius' (95). He explains Dryden's attacks on his inferior rival Elkanah Settle as an instance of 'malignant impatience' (84) which, in its low literary quality, exposed Dryden's disordered passions: 'minds are not levelled in their powers but when they are first levelled in their desires. Dryden and Settle had both placed their happiness in the claps of multitudes' (87–8). To fully understand Dryden's work, then, the words on the page will not suffice: you need to see the man behind them.

Johnson also has a more general moral lesson to impart. The *Lives* is too diffuse a work to have an overriding message, but one of its consistent themes is the writerly tendency to self-aggrandizement, showing off, and a refusal to be normal. As one of Johnson's sermons observes, 'There is perhaps no class of men' so liable to be 'wise in their own conceits' as writers (*Works*, XIV.88). This is a moral fault with literary consequences, since 'whatever is improper or vicious, is produced by a voluntary deviation from nature in pursuit of something new and strange; and . . . writers fail to give delight, by their desire of exciting admiration' ('Life of Cowley', *Lives*, I.214).

When Johnson calls Milton 'naturally a thinker for himself' (*Lives*, I.294–5), this is not just a compliment. The words 'singular' and 'peculiar' recur in the 'Life of Swift', always with a disapproving tone. Poets are the kind of people who should be brought back down to earth – which is one of the *Lives*' functions. There is little idealism here about the literary life – a life which, Johnson implies in the 'Life of West', is unlikely to stand one in good stead on the Day of Judgement: 'a stroke of the palsy brought to the grave one of the few poets to whom the grave might be without its terrors' (*Lives*, IV.118).

As in the *Life of Savage*, Johnson restores the balance by bringing 'mankind' into the picture – or at least, that part of mankind which pays attention to literature. Repeatedly, Johnson gives the audience the final word in critical judgement, as a remedy against writers' individualism.[6] And he hints that the audience will also have the last word on the *Lives of the Poets* itself. The 'Life of Pope' implies that the reader may be able to detect the faults of the work – 'if the reader should suspect me, as I suspect myself, of some partial fondness for the memory of Dryden' (*Lives*, IV.66) – and Johnson's brief introduction to the 'Life of Young', which Johnson farmed out to Herbert Croft, jokes that the *Lives* might have been improved if Croft had written even more of them (IV.132). As in the *Rambler*, Johnson undermines his own prose in order to give readers their due.

Beyond Moralism

Johnson's work often introduces other forms of judgement alongside the moral kind. He is, for instance, interested in the questions which writers like to discuss among themselves. The 'Life of Dryden' is full of them. How diligently did Dryden edit his own poetry, and was anyone even more thorough (*Lives*, II.108)? If criticizing someone else's translation, how can you show you are being fair (107)? What is the smart response when one is accused of plagiarism (100)?

Sometimes these issues are raised without any ethical implications; they are, rather, part of the overriding question of how to survive and succeed in the literary world. But morality is always breaking in. Pope, when attacked by Cibber, could have kept his dignity by remaining silent. 'But Pope's irascibility prevailed' (*Lives*, IV.50). That was an error of public relations strategy, but also a revelation that Pope had not mastered his passions. Similarly, the *Lives* are interested in how literary talent is misdirected or squandered, and this can reflect badly on a writer's character. Rochester did not make enough of 'a mind which study might have carried to excellence. What more can be expected from a life spent in ostentatious contempt of regularity ... ?' ('Life of Rochester', *Lives*, II.14).

As we have seen, the *Life of Savage* concludes in a similarly blunt judgement about its subject's 'irregularity'. Was that a cold way to treat a friend? *Rambler* 60 in effect answered that question:

> If the biographer writes from personal knowledge, and makes haste to gratify the publick curiosity, there is danger lest his interest, his fear, his gratitude, or his tenderness, overpower his fidelity, and tempt him to conceal, if not to invent. There are many who think it an act of piety to hide the faults or failings of their friends, even when they can no longer suffer by their detection; we therefore see whole ranks of characters adorned with uniform panegyrick, and not to be known from one another, but by extrinsick and casual circumstances. 'Let me remember', says Hale, 'when I find myself inclined to pity a criminal, that there is likewise a pity due to the country.' If we owe regard to the memory of the dead, there is yet more respect to be paid to knowledge, to virtue, and to truth. (*Works*, III.323)

If Johnson could take this approach to Savage, then of course he could write with equal bluntness of, say, Waller, who of all the major figures in the *Lives* receives the harshest judgements. '[M]ore than sixty years had not been able to teach him morality' (*Lives*, II.48). But the *Life of Savage* also hints at a different rhetorical mode, one which would take shape fully in the *Lives of the Poets*.

It was, he writes, 'in no time of Mr. Savage's life any part of his character to be the first of the company that desired to separate' (*Lives*, III.133). In other words, Savage was an irresponsible heavy drinker who never knew when it was time to go home. But Johnson does not use those other words; he employs more teasing ones instead. This tone, which only appears fleetingly in the *Life of Savage*, becomes a mainstay of the *Lives of the Poets*. Here he is on Thomson's overvaluing his poem *Liberty*: 'Upon this great poem two years were spent, and the author congratulated himself upon it as his noblest work; but an author and his reader are not always of a mind' (*Lives*, IV.99). This understated ridicule is, for Johnson, a gentler and kinder way to deflate literary vanity. The 'Life of Waller' enjoys Waller's failure to woo an aristocratic lady with love poetry; when Waller later marries someone else, Johnson remarks that 'It has not been discovered that this wife was won by his poetry' (*Lives*, II.30). Behind the irony is a broader point: literary excellence may be of little use in the world, because even this world's standards – let alone those of Almighty God – are on a different plane from literary-critical judgements.

The 'Life of Milton'

In the 'Life of Milton', the most fully developed example of Johnson's biographical style, judgement and irony are both fully present, along with another quality: mercy. First, the judgement. Johnson presents Milton as an image of the proud writer: he 'loves himself rather than truth' (*Lives*, I.252) and is prey to 'prepossessions' and 'fancies'. Such delusional arrogance expresses itself in rebellious politics, the result of 'pride disdainful of superiority' (I.276).

Yet Johnson also employs more indirect, ironic means to put Milton in his place. He remarks, for instance, that Milton assumed a single word of his praise was 'a certain preservative from oblivion' (246). He draws the reader's attention, firmly if undemonstratively, to the occasions when Milton looks a little absurd: disputing grammatical niceties in the middle of a political debate, for example, and ending up in 'slavery' to Cromwell's wishes. And a celebrated paragraph enjoys the spectacle of Milton's return to the country as the dispute between Charles I and Parliament heats up – only to spend his time, anticlimactically enough, running a small school:

> Let not our veneration for Milton forbid us to look with some degree of merriment on great promises and small performance, on the man who hastens home, because his countrymen are contending for their liberty, and, when he reaches the scene of action, vapours away his patriotism in a private boarding-school. This is the period of his life from which all his biographers seem inclined to shrink. (*Lives*, I.248)

Yet as in the *Life of Savage*, Johnson is prepared to plead for his subject – though, notably, it is usually when Milton is being shown in some humiliated state. So, he refers to Milton as a 'great man' (I.262) – but only at the moment of Milton's fall from grace, when the king returns. After Milton's reputation recovers despite this blow, Johnson observes: 'Such is the reverence paid to great abilities, however misused' (269). Having outlined the misuse, Johnson is prepared to join in with the reverence. Eventually, he writes of Milton's 'multiplicity of attainments, and extent of comprehension, that entitle this great author to our veneration'; but he is only able to praise Milton like this because he has just found in the poet, paradoxically enough, 'a kind of humble dignity' (272).

At one moment in the 'Life of Milton', Johnson gives us a glimpse of his biographical principles. When explaining the authorities' merciful treatment of Milton at the Restoration, he writes: 'He was now poor and blind; and who would pursue with violence an illustrious enemy, depressed by fortune, and disarmed by nature?' (263). There is something unseemly about 'pursuing with violence' someone who is already suffering. And on Johnson's view of human life, everyone can be counted in that category; so the biographer, however much he wants to puncture his subject's arrogance and instruct his readers, has to show mercy.

In his 'Life of Ascham', Johnson passes over Ascham's faults lightly on the grounds that 'It were indecent to treat with wanton levity the memory of a man who shared his frailties with all, but whose learning or virtues few can attain' (*Works*, XIX.444). A strikingly similar phrase appears in *Rasselas*, when Imlac tells his companions, with reference to the astronomer who has lost his wits: 'to mock the heaviest of human afflictions is neither charitable nor wise. Few can attain this man's knowledge, and few practise his virtues; but all may suffer his calamity' (*Works*, XVI.149). The learned and brilliant, the people who get biographies written of them, may seem out of the ordinary; but in their vulnerability to misfortune, they are just like us.

Figure 8.1 Johnson about 1783 by John Opie.
Courtesy of Houghton Library, Harvard University (82M-20).

Chapter 8

Legend

> I hope the day will never arrive when I shall neither be the object of calumny or ridicule, for then I shall be neglected and forgotten.
> (*Miscellanies*, II.420)

Once upon a time, Johnson's personality had to be guessed at from his writings. The teenage Bennet Langton, an admirer of the *Rambler* essays, went to London in the mid-1750s to meet its author. He expected to find

> a decent, well-drest, in short, a remarkably decorous philosopher. Instead of which, down from his bed-chamber, about noon, came, as newly risen, a huge uncouth figure, with a little dark wig which scarcely covered his head, and his clothes hanging loose about him. But his conversation was so rich, so animated, and so forcible, and his religious and political notions so congenial . . . that he [Langton] conceived for him that veneration and attachment which he ever preserved. (*Life*, I.247–8)

Langton became a lifelong friend. But reconciling Johnson the writer and Johnson the man was always a struggle. It was James Boswell who brought the two Johnsons together in one monumental book, the *Life of Samuel Johnson*. Any discussion of Johnson's reception is to some extent a dialogue with this book; however much you try to escape from Boswell – and there are good reasons to try, as we will see – the extraordinary vividness of his account makes it impossible to ignore.

In a way, it is strange that Boswell emerged as the most influential biographer of Johnson. He spent (at a maximum estimate) 425 days with him, and only knew him in the last 21 years of his life.[1] Compare another of Johnson's biographers, John Hawkins: Hawkins knew Johnson from the early days on the *Gentleman's Magazine*, was a founding member of the Ivy Lane Club and the Literary Club, and was one of the three executors of Johnson's will (which does not mention Boswell). Hawkins's biography has been frequently disparaged – not entirely unjustly – ever since it came out, as a drab, carping work; but its author knew Johnson intimately, and his book often shows it. He is able, for instance, to reflect on how Johnson's demeanour became less arrogant over time. By the mid 1760s, he claims, Johnson

> had seen enough of the world to know, that respect was not to be extorted, and began now to be satisfied with that degree of eminence to which his writings had exalted him. This change in his behaviour was remarked by those who were best acquainted with his character, and it rendered him an easy and delightful companion.[2]

Someone else who knew Johnson better than Boswell ever did was Hester Thrale – Hester Piozzi, as she would become in 1784 by a marriage which Johnson disapproved of so strongly that it ended their nineteen-year friendship. Piozzi's *Anecdotes of Dr Johnson*, a record of that friendship, showed a Johnson different to Boswell's – less competitive, less intimidating, more vulnerable, though just as capable of indefensible behaviour: 'one day at dinner I meant to please Mr. Johnson particularly with a dish of very young peas. "Are not they charming?" said I to him, while he was eating them. "Perhaps", said he, "they would be so—to a *pig*" (*Miscellanies*, I.190). But in Piozzi's book, Johnson – unlike in Boswell's where he is so often on his guard – relaxes more and sometimes reveals his emotional vulnerability. Piozzi can tell the reader, for instance, that Nekayah's reflections in *Rasselas* on family discord 'took their source from its author's keen recollections of the time passed in his early years'; and that Johnson 'burst into a passion of tears one day' when reading aloud the passage in *The Vanity of Human Wishes* about the disappointments of a scholar's life (*Miscellanies*, I.151, 180). While Boswell preserves intact a great treasury of stories and remarks, Piozzi can sit back and generalize about Johnson's habits of mind:

> when he talked of authors, his praise went spontaneously to such passages as are sure in his own phrase to leave something behind them useful on common occasions, or observant of common manners ... It was not King Lear cursing his daughters, or deprecating the storm, that I remember his commendations of; but Iago's ingenious malice, and subtle revenge; or prince Hal's gay compliance with Falstaff, whom he all along despised. (*Miscellanies*, I.282–3)

In addition to the major biographies, many shorter and more routine pieces were published soon after Johnson's death, by authors including Joseph Towers and William Shaw. The stream has never stopped – in Johnson's tercentenary year of 2009, three full-length biographies appeared. Johnson fascinated his contemporaries as he has fascinated posterity. Then as now, not all the attention was friendly.

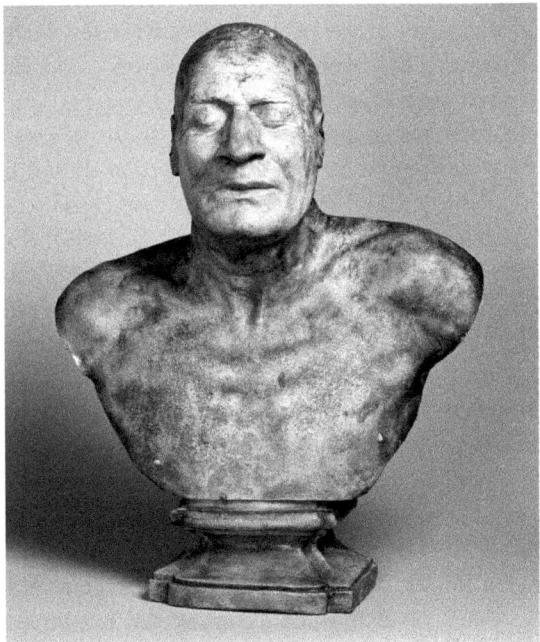

Figure 8.2 Johnson's death mask, after William Cumberland Cruikshank. © National Portrait Gallery, London.

'Pomposo'

Johnson was buried in Westminster Abbey on 20 December 1784; twelve years later, a sizeable marble statue was put up in St Paul's Cathedral. During his lifetime, Johnson had already become a monument – and monuments are easy targets. Of his thousands of appearances in the London press during his lifetime, 'Many of the notices are friendly', writes E. A. Bloom, but 'more are hostile if not downright venomous.'[3] The topics of the hostility and venom became familiar ones: that Johnson was self-important, short-tempered, envious of his fellow writers, and a political sell-out (thanks to his pension). John Wiltshire has shown that, from early on, Johnson's critics picked on his unusual appearance to characterize him as monstrous, inhuman.[4] Charles Churchill's *The Ghost*, whose portrait of 'Pomposo' set the tone for much subsequent abuse, described him as 'Not quite a *Beast*, nor quite a *Man*,/ Like – God knows what'.[5] When in 1782 John Callender brought out a spiteful anthology, *Deformities of Dr Johnson*, an anonymous critic for the *Monthly Review* sighed at the unoriginality of the project: there were few blemishes 'in this literary luminary that have not been discovered before', and Callender's project displayed more 'malignity' than 'wit'.[6]

Johnson usually welcomed the insults: 'Why now, these fellows are only advertising my book (he would say); it is surely better a man should be abused than forgotten' (*Miscellanies*, I.270–1). He was at first displeased when James Barclay defended him publicly against a bad review (*Life*, I.498). *Rambler* 93 had argued: 'he that writes may be considered as a kind of general challenger, whom every one has a right to attack; since he quits the common rank of life, steps forward beyond the lists, and offers his merit to the publick judgment' (*Works*, IV.133–4). But Johnson's friends did feel the need to defend him – especially after his death when, as Samuel Parr observed, 'Now that the old lion is dead, every ass thinks he may kick at him' (*Life*, IV.423). The *Prayers and Meditations*, published a year after his death, did not help: these private religious reflections were seen as embarrassingly intimate, sometimes neurotic – in Johnson's little self-denials like not putting milk in tea on Good Friday – and even superstitious: praying for the dead, as Johnson did for Tetty, was seen as scandalously Roman Catholic (even though Johnson did it somewhat hesitantly). The recent memory of Johnson's *Lives of the Poets*, whose treatments of Milton and Gray in particular had irritated many readers, did not help. The anti-Johnsonian bandwagon rolled on.

Piozzi's *Anecdotes of Dr Johnson* (1786) often showed Johnson at his harsh, inflexible worst. Piozzi frankly admitted that 'When I relate these various instances of contemptuous behaviour shewn to a variety of people, I am aware that those who till now have heard little of Mr. Johnson will here cry out against his pride and his severity' (*Miscellanies*, I.296). But, she added significantly, his harshness never expressed itself in deeds: 'all he did was gentle, if all he said was rough'.

Even the most hostile authors, by their evident compulsion to have a crack at Johnson, were paying him a sort of accidental compliment. It was not until 1791, however, seven years after his death, that a tribute arrived on such a scale as almost to obscure Johnson himself.

Boswell

In 1762, James Boswell came down from Scotland to London. He was romantic in his politics, intermittently fervent in his religion, and famously wayward in his love life. But perhaps his most long-standing passion was for Samuel

Johnson, whom he met on 16 May 1763, in the back of Tom Davies's bookshop in Covent Garden: 'The single event from which modern biography sprang', one present-day practitioner of the genre has written.[7] From the start, Boswell recorded the smallest details, hoping to present the most complete picture possible. Some readers felt that Boswell was irresponsibly revealing – though, in fact, he suppressed quite a lot in order to protect Johnson and others.

Boswell intruded himself into the story, but only to bring Johnson more vividly into the foreground: he would cheerfully record episodes which made Boswell himself look foolish. One was that first meeting, where Johnson immediately insulted Boswell for being a Scot. A few minutes later Boswell put his foot in it by commenting on Johnson's friendship with David Garrick and received a 'stern look' and a sharp putdown. 'I now felt myself much mortified', Boswell recalled, 'and began to think that the hope which I had long indulged of obtaining his acquaintance was blasted' (*Life*, I.394–5).

But Boswell persevered, and a month later, Johnson was asking why he didn't see him more often:

> Trusting that I was now in his good graces, I answered, that he had not given me much encouragement, and reminded him of the check I had received from him at our first interview. 'Poh, Poh! (said he, with a complacent smile,) never mind these things. Come to me as often as you can. I shall be glad to see you.' (*Life*, I.399)

From his journal, Boswell built his life's work: 'I have a constant plan', he wrote in March 1772, 'to write the life of Mr Johnson. I have not told him of it yet, nor do I know if I should tell him.'[8] The following year, he and Johnson visited Scotland together, and Boswell's record of that trip – a precursor to the *Life* – was published a year after Johnson's death.

Boswell's research was assiduous, even though he was sometimes mistaken. After Johnson's death, he took over six years to bring together his notes, as well as the letters, stories, and facts he had collected, and then edit them into some kind of narrative. The result is hardly a textbook example of biography. But it is a terrific read, as generations of admirers can attest; and the main reason is that it gives us Johnson at first hand, as though we were in the same room.

> The mention of the wolf had led Johnson to think of other wild beasts; and while Sir Joshua Reynolds and Mr. Langton were carrying on a dialogue about something which engaged them earnestly, he, in the midst of it, broke out, 'Pennant tells of Bears – ' (what he added, I have forgotten.) They went on, which he being dull of hearing, did not perceive, or, if he

did, was not willing to break off his talk; so he continued to vociferate his remarks, and *Bear* ('like a word in a catch', as Beauclerk said,) was repeatedly heard at intervals, which coming from him who, by those who did not know him, had been so often assimilated [compared] to that ferocious animal, while we who were sitting around could hardly stifle laughter, produced a very ludicrous effect. Silence having ensued, he proceeded: 'We are told, that the black bear is innocent; but I should not like to trust myself with him.' Mr. Gibbon muttered, in a low tone of voice, 'I should not like to trust myself with *you*.' (*Life*, II.347–8)

Johnson's conversational fluency and pointedness are famous mainly thanks to Boswell, who recorded such moments as this:

I suggested a doubt, that if I were to reside in London, the exquisite zest with which I relished it in occasional visits might go off, and I might grow tired of it. JOHNSON. 'Why, Sir, you find no man, at all intellectual, who is willing to leave London. No, Sir, when a man is tired of London, he is tired of life; for there is in London all that life can afford.' (*Life*, III.177–8)

Here we have to tread carefully. In his journal, Boswell noted Johnson saying only: 'You find no man wishes to leave it.' Such discrepancies between the *Life* and the journal are common. It is possible, of course, that Boswell's memory was so good that he only needed a rough note in the journal. But we cannot simply take him as an infallible transcriber.

Boswell's book has been called 'the first truly profound life of a writer's mind'.[9] Its accumulation of small details, the author's literary skill in bringing them together, and the love of his subject which illuminates the whole work, have so captivated readers that there has developed what one critic termed the 'Double Tradition of Dr. Johnson'.[10] Half the tradition relates to Johnson the author; the other half to a legendary figure, best known for his take-no-prisoners repartee. The 'popular' half of the tradition has often been a distortion, and Boswell has sometimes been blamed for foisting it upon the world. As has been pointed out already, Boswell was not Johnson's closest friend, nor did they spend a huge amount of time together. They were certainly not inseparable (though Johnson did write to him: 'I hold you as Hamlet has it, "in my heart of heart"', *Life*, II.384). Boswell's was a selective portrait; and given the scale of his influence, it may be worth looking a little more closely at how certain aspects of Boswell's *Life* subtly misrepresent Johnson. One important example, which several critics have recently observed, is that Boswell tends to overlook Johnson's role as a supporter of women writers and even something of a proto-feminist.

Throughout the Romantic era – when Johnson's literary reputation, as we will see, took a nosedive – his works were nevertheless 'much read and respected by women, who often found them useful for their own writings'.[11] Not the least of these was Mary Wollstonecraft, who included five extracts from Johnson in *The Female Reader*, maybe the first feminist anthology.[12] The early Spanish feminist Inés Joyes y Blake translated *Rasselas* into Spanish: she published the translation alongside 'Apologia de las mugeres' (1798), an argument for women to take up traditionally male studies – which was appropriate, since *Rasselas* ends with Nekayah announcing her plan to found a women's college.[13]

Frances Reynolds was understating the case when she said Johnson 'set a higher value on female friendship than, perhaps, most men' (*Miscellanies*, II.252). Among those female friends were many writers, to whom he gave practical and moral support, offering his collaboration, writing prefaces and dedications, and raising subscriptions. In 1750, he threw an all-night party for Charlotte Lennox to celebrate her first novel; thirty-one years later, he was asking a friend to visit this 'great Genius', who had fallen on hard times (*Letters*, III.353–4). He helped many women gain connections in the literary world; read drafts and gave comments to authors including Frances Reynolds and Hannah More; collaborated on a translation of Boethius with Hester Thrale (as she then was), stopping only because a poorer translator was about to put his own effort on the market.[14] His most significant mentee was born too late to meet him: Jane Austen called 'my dear Dr Johnson' her favourite prose moralist, and his irony as well as his ethical seriousness are major influences on Austen's novels.[15]

Put all that together, and Johnson becomes a serious candidate for one of the first modern feminists – except that, on other occasions, he spoke exactly like a man of his time. As we have seen, Johnson's social and political thought prized the security of the social order; and this included double standards about relations between the sexes. He reckoned men committed adultery because their wives were 'negligent of pleasing' (*Life*, II.56). As Hester Thrale Piozzi, who should have known, commented, 'He did indeed say very contemptuous things of our sex' (*Miscellanies*, I.327). That is enough to temper some of the larger claims made about Johnson's feminism; still, these were remarks in conversation, often deliberately overstated, and should be weighed against all Johnson's other statements and the demonstrable facts of his life.

That brings us to another way in which Boswell skews the picture: his most memorable passages are of Johnson in conversation, often answering Boswell's own provocative questions. He therefore seems to be acting a part – the great sage and wit – which inevitably grows tedious if it is abstracted from the thinking, living, suffering, and often solitary man behind the one-liners. He becomes a sort of panel-show comedian, expected to have an answer to everything, or a monopolizer of conversation: Boswell will sometimes rearrange a dialogue between the two of them as if it had been a monologue from Johnson. Because he cuts out the passages when Johnson says nothing, we forget Johnson's comment that 'Tom Tyers described me the best. He once said to me, "Sir, (said he,) you are like a ghost: you never speak till you are spoken to"' (*Life*, V.73). (Though, to be fair, Boswell recorded that very remark.)

Thanks to these distortions, Johnson is widely remembered as a dictatorial figure and something of a pub bore. 'A good talk', for Johnson, meant real discussion – and he was prepared to be confrontational in the course of it. So, Boswell's biography, which focuses disproportionately on Johnson the talker, has also entrenched the notion of Johnson as belligerent, haughty, and painfully direct. One story, in particular, has helped this side of his character to dominate the Johnson legend. Asked by Boswell about Bishop Berkeley's theory that things only exist insofar as they are perceived, Johnson kicked a large stone and announced 'I refute it *thus*' (*Life*, I.471). Critics have defended the act as more thoughtful than it looks: it can be read as expressing Thomas Reid's philosophy of perception, or David Hartley's theory of touch.[16] Whether or not one buys that kind of interpretation, it is certain that Johnson had a good grasp of philosophical matters, and that the image of a philistine trying to refute a philosopher by rugged common sense gets Johnson all wrong. Iris Murdoch writes in an aside that 'clearly Dr Johnson, when he refuted Berkeley by kicking a stone, had not "really tried" to understand Berkeley'.[17] But *Idler* 10 refers to Berkeley's followers as having 'the honour at least of being deceived by fallacies not easily detected' (*Works*, II.33). Johnson disagreed with Berkeley but respected him. He did not ban quotations of Berkeley from his *Dictionary*, as he did Hobbes and Samuel Clarke. Yet taken in isolation, the famous refutation gives a false impression that Johnson was a proud know-nothing, the kind of person who thinks all these philosophers are just playing with language.

At the same time, Johnson was capable of a brutally oversimplifying verbal riposte: when Hugh Blair, defending the (supposedly ancient) Ossian poems against the charge of being a hoax, asked whether any modern man could have written the poems, Johnson replied: 'Yes, Sir, many men, many women, and many children' (*Life*, I.396). And though Johnson turned out to be right about Ossian, some of his other thumping put-downs sound less impressive. 'Sir (said he,) we *know* our will is free, and *there's* an end on't' (*Life*, II.82): it's a memorable formulation, but it hardly resolves the issue.

Boswell's account, then, sometimes promotes half-truths. And the editing of Boswell's manuscript of the *Life* by Marshall Waingrow, Bruce Redford, and Thomas Bonnell has revealed that it strays from accuracy. But as Waingrow himself graciously put it, with an allusion to one of Johnson's own critical principles: 'no matter how many new facts are brought to light, Samuel Johnson will always be somebody's hypothesis. And none has pleased so many, or is likely to please so long, as Boswell's.'[18]

Nevertheless, Boswell's account needs to be constantly brought into contact with those of others and with Johnson's writings. Hazlitt's assertion that 'The most triumphant record of the talents and character of Johnson is to be found in Boswell's Life of him. The man was superior to the author' falls short, not only because it takes Johnson lightly as a thinker and writer, but because it puts too much trust in Boswell.[19] Yet when Hazlitt made that sweeping judgement, he was speaking for many members of his generation.

The Romantic Reaction

Several of the major writers in the half-century after Johnson's death – Coleridge, Keats, Hazlitt, Blake, to an extent Wordsworth – disliked Johnson, in some cases with a curious intensity. The familiar criticisms returned, expressed with the familiar venom. Keats scribbled rude remarks on his copy of Johnson's Shakespeare criticism.[20] Coleridge planned an essay 'on the supposed Genius, Style, critical powers, & morals, of Dr. S. Johnson' – and given Coleridge's general loathing of Johnson, the key word is 'supposed'.[21] Hazlitt told the reader of *Characters of Shakespear's Plays*: 'If Dr Johnson's opinion was right, [Hazlitt's] observations on Shakespear's plays must be greatly exaggerated, if not ridiculous.'[22]

James Boulton writes of 'the Romantics' realization that Johnson epitomized supremely the assumptions about man, nature, and human life which had to be rejected if their own were to prevail ... Johnson provided a sacrificial victim essential to the success of the literary and moral revolution'.[23] That 'revolution', inasmuch as it can be summarized, upheld principles which could scarcely coexist with Johnson's: the elevation of art to a quasi-religion; the focus on the personality of the artist; the emphasis on emotional experience over ethical codes.[24] While those ideals were in the ascendant, Johnson went out of fashion. There were exceptions. Mary Shelley wrote, 'I do love the kind hearted wise and Gentle Bear – & think him as loveable a (man) friend as a profound philosopher.'[25] Byron praised Johnson; but he did so with a consciousness that he was swimming against the tide. Most of Romanticism's major figures either disputed Johnson's authority or – just as significantly – had little to say about him.

Popular taste disagreed. *Rasselas* and *The Rambler* were constantly republished in the late eighteenth and early nineteenth centuries; even so, by the late 1820s, the Romantics had helped Johnson's stock to decline.[26] Meanwhile, the continued popularity of Boswell's *Life* had mixed implications for Johnson's standing. In 1831, John Wilson Croker produced a new edition of Boswell, reviewed in style by Lord Macaulay. Macaulay was out to humiliate Croker, a political opponent, and while arraigning the edition for its inaccuracy and poor presentation, he also mocked Boswell and offered a vivid but misleading portrait of Johnson. Croker reportedly found the piece 'a damned nuisance'.[27] not a few Johnsonians since would have nodded sadly along to that judgement. Macaulay's essay had a major and largely unfortunate impact.[28] He wrote as though intoxicated by his own superb prose, throwing out half-truths or total distortions. Macaulay asserted, for instance, that Johnson had a contempt for foreign travel. G. B. Hill pointed out in 1878 that Macaulay had taken one remark out of context, misquoted it, and overlooked passage after passage which told against his generalization. At Oxford, Johnson had longed to visit Italy, and he still talked excitedly of the idea in his sixties; he wished aloud that he could visit the Great Wall of China.[29] According to Hester Thrale Piozzi, 'His desire to go abroad, particularly to see Italy, was very great, and he had a longing wish too to leave some Latin verses at the Grand Chartreux. He loved indeed the very act of travelling' (*Miscellanies*, I.263).

Macaulay had repeatedly made similar mistakes. But as Hill lamented, Macaulay's essays 'are read in every quarter of the world. They have been sold by thousands and tens of thousands, and wherever they are read a grievous wrong is done to the memory of Johnson.'[30] These distortions mattered. And Macaulay's character-portrait of Johnson was a crude simplification, as an extract will show:

> The characteristic peculiarity of his intellect was the union of great powers with low prejudices ... Where he was not under the influence of some strange scruple, or some domineering passion, which prevented him from boldly and fairly investigating a subject, he was a wary and acute reasoner ... But, if while he was beating down sophisms and exposing false testimony, some childish prejudices, such as would excite laughter in a well managed nursery, came across him, he was smitten as if

by enchantment. His mind dwindled away under the spell from gigantic elevation to dwarfish littleness.[31]

Macaulay's paradox was not original. It is strikingly close to Horace Walpole's 1785 dismissal of Johnson's 'preposterous assemblage of strong sense, of the lowest bigotry and prejudices, of pride, brutality, fretfulness, and vanity'.[32] In 1792, a writer for the *Monthly Review* wrote: 'As often as he displays the singular magnitude of his mind, the man of genius will lament, and the man of common talents will exult, over the alloy which debased it.'[33] The 'alloy' was Johnson's unbecoming personal appearance and his 'odious' 'superstition and bigotry'. Macaulay gave this idea – the preposterous assemblage, the debased alloy – a forceful rhetorical push. His condescending tone worked its way into many other nineteenth-century judgements on Johnson. In 1884, on the centenary of Johnson's death, the *Times* remarked: 'The infatuate admiration which he inspired ... is not wholly comprehensible to this generation ... he cannot be ranked high as a philosopher or poet.'[34]

Leslie Stephen took the stone-kicking Johnson as the truest image of him, and in his 1876 *History of English Thought in the Eighteenth Century* patronized him as an anti-philosophical philistine: 'no man could care less for the foundations of speculative truth'.[35] Johnson's intellectual range and abilities were fair game, too, for Edmund Gosse in 1884: 'the writings yield to the personality ... Must we not admit now, at the close of a century, that it is practically impossible to read him?'[36]

It is Macaulay's Johnson, as much as anyone else's, who appears in a 1987 episode of the television comedy *Blackadder*. Though the characters refer to Johnson as 'the cleverest man in England', he is still a pitifully narrow-minded man, unable to speak except in pointlessly wordy sentences and losing his temper at the slightest challenge.[37] He is an overgrown toddler, just as Macaulay had described him 150 years previously.

Nineteenth-Century Mythologies

For all its influence, Macaulay's essay did not single-handedly define Johnson for the nineteenth-century reader. Johnson's works – not just Boswell's *Life* – were widely read. There were over twenty editions of *Rasselas* between 1837 and 1900.[38] Victorian authors were far friendlier to Johnson than the Romantics: as Katherine Turner has observed, the Brownings, Charlotte Brontë, John Ruskin, and George Eliot all admired Johnson; and he must have had some marketability for Matthew Arnold to publish a selection from

The Lives of the Poets to help fund his retirement.[39] As English Literature became institutionalized in the latter part of the Victorian era, Johnsons' position in the canon was assured.

Even so, Johnson the author was a smaller figure than Johnson the man. If 'The Age of Johnson' had become a common designation at this time, Johnson was seen as age-defining less because of his writings and more because his character seemed to express other things: Englishness, Augustanism, 'the Hero as Man of Letters'.[40] That last phrase was Thomas Carlyle's, whose own review of Croker exalted Johnson. In his lectures *On Heroes, Hero-Worship and the Heroic in History*, published in 1841, Carlyle rises to offer a heartfelt eulogy:

> Johnson's Writings, which once had such currency and celebrity, are now, as it were, disowned by the younger generation. It is not wonderful; Johnson's opinions are fast becoming obsolete: but his style of thinking and of living, we may hope, will never become obsolete. I find in Johnson's Books the indisputable traces of a great intellect and a great heart ... They are *sincere* words, those of his; he means things by them ... Shall we not say, of this great mournful Johnson too, that he guided his difficult confused existence wisely; led it *well*, like a right-valiant man?[41]

Like Macaulay – though with rather more intellectual integrity – Carlyle privileged the man over the thinker: Johnson's opinions were 'obsolete', but Johnson himself was magnetic as an example of courage and honesty. His life was an example for the rest of us to look up to: as Walter Jackson Bate would put it in his 1975 biography, 'he had proved that it was possible to get through this strange adventure of life, and to do it in a way that is a tribute to human nature'.[42] It helped Carlyle's case that, thanks to Boswell, Johnson's life was so full of colour and character and laughter. So, in the nineteenth century, Johnson became a popular icon. A mythology grew up around the great scenes of his life, and many artworks depicted these moments.

The price of this fame was inaccuracy. In the Market Square at Lichfield, a massive statue of Johnson, erected in 1838, has three Johnsonian scenes around its base. Unfortunately, one of them – Johnson being carried by his schoolmates – is a misinterpretation of a story from Boswell; another, Johnson listening to Dr Sacheverell preaching, is probably apocryphal. The Johnson legend had developed a life of its own.

It is easy to mock, but Johnson had only achieved his fame because so many people could not get him out of their heads. Sometimes 'Dr Johnson' eclipsed his works; but some readers profited from the writings precisely because of the compelling personality they found within them. Ruskin recalled in his autobiography how Johnson's essays had strengthened him 'against all chance of being misled by my own sanguine and metaphysical temperament ... he saved me for ever from false thoughts and futile speculations'.[43]

Besides, the mythology sometimes reflected deeper truths. For instance, the popular image of Johnson has him fixed as an old man. This is partly down to historical accident. As John Wiltshire notes, James Barry's 1778–80 portrait of Johnson around the age of seventy became the model for many other artistic representations. Edward Matthew Ward's *Doctor Johnson in the Ante-Room of the Lord Chesterfield Waiting for an Audience* shows a figure very like Barry's, although when Johnson sat in Lord Chesterfield's anteroom he was actually in his late thirties. The early-middle-aged Johnson is absorbed by the old man.[44] A travesty of history, then – but perhaps it pays an unconscious tribute to Johnson's gift for reflecting on the complexity of human life without sounding blasé. The insights of his writing seem to spring from hard-won experience; the image of old age is partly an image of wisdom.

Boswell had another boost when G. B. Hill published his 1887 six-volume edition of the *Life*, with illustrations and copious notes; in its 1934 revision by L. F. Powell, it remains the standard edition. Hill's devotion and labour helped to confirm the significance of Boswell's work; and indeed, Hill thought that Boswell was more worth reading than Johnson. But Hill was also helping to usher in a new age of Johnson scholarship which would call into question that judgement.

Taking Johnson Seriously

'Never was there a more ignorant fable than the fable which makes Boswell the creator of Johnson's greatness.'[45] Walter Raleigh's blunt verdict, delivered in his 1910 *Six Essays on Johnson*, helped initiate the creative destruction of nineteenth-century mythology. Raleigh acknowledged that we owe 'an enormous debt of gratitude to Boswell' and argued that the reader of Johnson would gain a great deal from being steeped in the *Life*: 'Any reader who acquaints himself intimately with the records of Johnson's life, and then reads *The Rambler*, must be very insensible if he does not find it one of the most moving of books.'[46] Life and works, for Raleigh, were inseparable. But he warned that, of Johnson's many admirers, 'some of them perhaps are worshippers rather than lovers, and lovers rather than friends. At any rate, they do not read his works.'[47] Raleigh ended his book by predicting that Johnson's writings would come back into fashion. He was right, and by taking Johnson's criticism seriously – for the first time since Matthew Arnold – he helped to make it happen.[48] Scholarly interest in Johnson steadily grew over the next half-century and has never died away. The *Yale Edition of the Works of Samuel Johnson*, conceived in 1951 as an attempt to preserve Johnson's writings as well as his persona, was finally completed in 2018. Meanwhile, there have been important Oxford editions of the *Lives*, the *Journey*, and the *Poems*; an *Oxford Handbook*, a revised *Cambridge Companion*, and a *Longman's Annotated English Poets* edition of Johnson have recently appeared; and an attempt is at last well under way to edit the *Dictionary* in full.

Johnson was fortunate in his twentieth-century advocates. T. S. Eliot, who also noted how much Johnson had been distanced from his writings, affirmed that Johnson's criticism had unique insight. Yes, Johnson sometimes seems blind to the features which modern readers admire; but by the same token, 'Again and again, when he calls attention to beauties or to blemishes in the work of the poets of whom he writes, we must acknowledge that he is right, and that he is pointing out something that we might not have noticed independently.'[49] Like Raleigh, Eliot predicted that Johnson would come in from the cold: 'It remains to be seen whether the literary influence of Johnson ... does not merely await a generation which has not yet been born to receive it.'[50]

F. R. Leavis was another critic who helped Johnson's status. He, too, complained that 'In this country, to those seriously interested in literature, the cult of Johnson is an exasperation and a challenge ... Johnson, one finds oneself having again and again to insist, was not only the Great Clubman; he was a great writer and a great highbrow.'[51] Leavis referred repeatedly to the 'weight' of Johnson's words. 'Johnson's criticism', he once wrote, 'is alive and life-giving' partly because of 'the weight that seems to be a matter of bringing to bear at every point the ordered experience of a lifetime'.[52] Leavis adopted Eliot's line that 'Johnson's limitations as a critic have positive correlatives'.[53] He also helped to overturn the tempting, but lazy, notion that Johnson specialized in lofty generalities. Rather, 'Johnson's abstractions and generalities are not mere empty explicitness substituting for the concrete; they focus a wide range of profoundly representative experience – experience felt by the reader as movingly present.'[54] A similar point was made at the same time by W. K. Wimsatt in *The Prose Style of Samuel Johnson*. Wimsatt demonstrated that Johnson's prose style was dense only because it was packed with thought and experience. Wimsatt was one of several critics who re-evaluated Johnson's writings and, by taking them seriously, enabled readers to see their significance. Johnson emerged as an important moralist and religious writer; his politics was seen as far more thoughtful than the bigoted-Tory image had allowed; his literary criticism was respected instead of being patronized.

It helped that many twentieth-century authors manifested a strong attachment to Johnson. Virginia Woolf, who put Johnson into *Orlando*, called him 'the stuff that Saints are made of ... one of the very few human beings who love their kind'.[55] She acknowledged that the Johnson 'myth' had inspired 'People who have never read a word of Johnson's writings'; at the same time, she praised 'the grace and elasticity of his style'[56] and gave a serious endorsement to Johnson's criticism by titling her essay collections *The Common Reader*. The epigraph was the celebrated sentence from the 'Life of Gray' (see Chapter 5): 'I rejoice to concur with the common reader; for by the common sense of readers uncorrupted with literary prejudices, after all the refinements of subtilty and the dogmatism of learning, must be finally decided all claim to poetical honours' (*Lives*, IV.184).

Many other major figures admired Johnson's work. Vladimir Nabokov shaped his novel *Pale Fire* around an extraordinary web of overt and covert Johnsonian references.[57] For G. K. Chesterton, who loved Johnson and wrote a play about him, it is the

> gigantic realism in Johnson's kindness, the directness of his emotionalism, when he is emotional, that gives him his hold upon generations of living men. There is nothing elaborate about his ethics; he wants to know whether a man, as a fact, is happy or unhappy, is lying or telling the truth. He may seem to be hammering at the brain through long nights of noise and thunder, but he can walk into the heart without knocking.[58]

A less predictable fan was Samuel Beckett: 'It's Johnson, always Johnson, who is with me. And if I follow any tradition, it is his.' He, too, saw past the Johnson myth:

> It isn't Boswell's wit and wisdom machine that means anything to me, but the miseries he never talked of, being unwilling or unable to do so. The horror of annihilation, the horror of madness, the horrified love of Mrs Thrale, the whole mental monster ridden swamp that after hours of silence could only give some ghastly bubble like 'Lord have mercy on us'.[59]

Beckett's emphasis, though a touch melodramatic, nevertheless exemplified something new in the twentieth century: the age of Freud and Jung began to read Johnson psychologically. He was seen as a precursor of psychoanalysis, above all in his accounts of repression – a force which could both help character development and stunt it – and in his many references to the power of something like the unconscious: for instance, 'a thousand secret and slight competitions, scarcely known to the mind upon which they operate' (*Idler* 23, *Works*, II.73).⁶⁰ Johnson's mind was also studied in psychoanalytic terms. Walter Jackson Bate's 1975 biography – one of a number of fine biographical studies in the last sixty years – identified in Johnson 'the almost desperate clutch outward to fact and objective reality of any sort in order to cleanse and free the dark subjective self – with all its frantic fears, and all its blind and destructive treacheries, including self-treachery'.⁶¹

So, we come back, via Johnson's works, to his life: but more recent biographies have acknowledged, as Walter Raleigh pointed out a century ago, that they often make most sense when viewed alongside each other.

The Future of Samuel Johnson

Academic fashions change, and Johnson probably attracts less attention today than thirty years ago. Yet he remains unignorable: a pillar of English Literature curricula all over the world, with a loyal readership outside the classroom too. Britain's former prime minister Boris Johnson believes that the country 'has never produced an author with a better or more generous understanding of human nature'.⁶² In 2020, another fan, the comedian Frank Skinner, co-presented a Sky Arts programme, *Boswell & Johnson's Scottish Road Trip*. Johnson is always popping up unexpectedly: he was quoted by both sides in Donald Trump's 2019 impeachment hearings, for instance.

Meanwhile, for those tempted to dismiss Johnson as the deadest of dead white European males, his excoriating writings on empire and slavery give him an urgent relevance in recent debates over history and racial justice. While a myth of European superiority was being built to justify ethnic cleansing and exploitation, Johnson exposed the cruelties of imperialism and wrote of the universality of the human race: 'wherever human nature is to be found, there is a mixture of vice and virtue, a contest of passion and reason; and … the Creator does not appear partial in his distributions' (*A Voyage to Abyssinia*, *Works*, XV.3–4). At around the same time as David Hume was writing contemptuously of non-white peoples – 'no ingenious manufactures amongst them, no arts, no sciences'⁶³ – Johnson was describing Egypt as 'a country famous among the earliest monarchies for the power and wisdom of its inhabitants; a country where the sciences first dawned that illuminate the world, and beyond which the arts cannot be traced of civil society or domestick life'⁶⁴ (*Rasselas*, *Works*, XVI.111).

Rambler 106 suggests that the author most likely to enjoy 'a long continuance of fame' is one 'who has carefully studied human nature, and can well describe it' (*Works*, IV.204). If Johnson seems more and more to have fulfilled that prescription, it is partly because he has been read and written about with so much intelligence and sensitivity. As Pat Rogers has said, 'We have learned not to mistake his fierce orthodoxy for unthinking conformism, or to misread his loyal Tory sentiments as the reflexes of a backwoods reactionary. Above all, we have learnt never to underrate the element of passion in his overtly rational world-view.'[65]

The other half of the 'Double Tradition' also lives on: a colossal mythology, the collective creation of hacks and geniuses, great critics and lazy journalists, none of it quite able to efface the life and works of Johnson himself. Wasn't the Literary Club growing a little stale, Oliver Goldsmith asked Johnson, now that they had travelled over each other's minds? If Boswell's account is to be believed, Johnson replied: 'Sir, you have not travelled over *my* mind, I promise you' (*Life*, IV.183).

Notes

1 Life and Times

1. See Michael Bundock, *The Fortunes of Francis Barber* (New Haven, CT: Yale University Press, 2015).

2 Journalist

1. Thomas Kaminski, *The Early Career of Samuel Johnson* (Oxford University Press, 1987), p. 5; *Life*, I.101n1.
2. Kaminski, p. 27.
3. Stephen Broadberry, Bruce S. M. Campbell, Alexander Klein, Mark Overton, and Bas van Leeuwen, *British Economic Growth, 1270–1870* (Cambridge University Press, 2015), p. 205.
4. Hawkins, Sir John, *The Life of Samuel Johnson, LL.D.*, ed. O. M. Brack (Athens: University of Georgia Press, 2009), p. 29.
5. Kaminski, pp. 165–8.
6. Thomas Babington Macaulay, *Critical, Historical and Miscellaneous Essays* (London, 1860), pp. 401–2.
7. Kaminski, p. 28.
8. Lawrence Lipking, *Samuel Johnson: The Life of an Author* (Cambridge, MA: Harvard University Press, 1998), p. 49.
9. Arthur Murphy, *Monthly Review* 76 (April 1787), p. 286.
10. *They Stand Together: The Letters of CS Lewis to Arthur Greeves 1914–1963*, ed. Walter Hooper (London: Harper Collins, 1979), p. 364.
11. John Wain, *Sprightly Running: Part of an Autobiography* (London: Macmillan, 1935), pp. 101–2.

3 Poet and Storyteller

1. Morris R. Brownell, *Samuel Johnson's Attitude to the Arts* (Oxford: Clarendon Press, 1989), pp. 8–34.

2. Lawrence Lipking, 'Learning to Read Johnson: "The Vision of Theodore" and the *Vanity of Human Wishes*', *ELH* 43, no. 4 (1976): 517–37.

4 Scholar

1. William Field, *Memoirs of the Life, Writings, and Opinions of the Rev. Samuel Parr, LL.D.*, 2 vols. (London: Henry Colburn, 1828), I.165.
2. These figures come from Brian Grimes, www.sjdictionarysources.org/.
3. Thomas Babington Macaulay, *Life of Samuel Johnson* (New York: Longmans, Green: 1896), p. 21.
4. BL Add MS 4254.

5 Critic

1. Harold Bloom, 'The Critic's Critic', *New York Times*, 5 November 2009.
2. *Shakespearean Criticism*, ed. T. M. Raysor, 2 vols. (London: Dent, 1960), I.215.
3. Raymond Williams, *Keywords* (New York: Oxford University Press, 1976), p. 219. Our treatment of 'nature' here draws on Robert DeMaria, Jr.'s chapter on the word in *English Literature 1640–1789: Keywords* (Oxford: Wiley-Blackwell, 2018).
4. Confirmed by Brian Grimes in personal communication. As we know that Johnson altered at least one of Reynolds's Discourses (*Bibliography* II.1559), it is tempting to suggest that the wording here is his in whole or in part.
5. See *Essays in the History of Ideas* (1948; rpt. Baltimore: Johns Hopkins University Press, 1982).
6. *The Diary of the Right Hon. William Windham 1784 to 1810*, ed. Mrs. Henry Baring (London: Longmans, Green and Co, 1866), p. 17.
7. *Lives*, IV.502 citing Lawrence Lipking, *The Ordering of the Arts in Eighteenth-Century England* (Princeton University Press, 1970), p. 454 and *Samuel Johnson: The Life of an Author* (Cambridge, MA: Harvard University Press, 1998), p. 263.

6 Social and Political Thinker

1. Nicholas Hudson, *Samuel Johnson and Eighteenth-Century Thought* (Oxford: Clarendon Press, 1988), pp. 184–9.
2. John Cannon, *Samuel Johnson and the Politics of Hanoverian England* (Oxford University Press, 1994), p. 155.

3. Simone Weil, *The Need for Roots* (London: Routledge and Kegan Paul, 1978), p. 13.
4. E.g. Sermon 23, *Works*, XIV.240.
5. *Letters and Prose Writings of William Cowper*, ed. James Kind and Charles Ryskamp (Oxford University Press, 1979–86), I.351.
6. Leslie Stephen, *English Thought in the 18th Century* (London: Smith, Elder & Co., 1881), II.206; quoted in Cannon, p. 113.
7. Anthony Pagden, *The Enlightenment: And Why It Still Matters* (Oxford University Press, 2013), p. 108.
8. Christopher Ricks, 'Literary Principles as Against Theory', in *Essays in Appreciation* (Oxford: Clarendon Press, 1996), pp. 311–33.
9. Nicholas Hudson, *A Political Biography of Samuel Johnson* (London: Pickering and Chatto, 2014), p. 100.
10. Hudson, *Political Biography*, p. 142.
11. *Boswell for the Defence*, ed. William K. Wimsatt and Frederick A. Pottle (New York: McGraw-Hill, 1959), p. 92.

7 Biographer

1. See *Works*, XIX.22.
2. See *Lives*, I.86.
3. See ibid., III.425n345.
4. See ibid., I.9, I.64–7.
5. See ibid., I. 86–95.
6. See ibid., II.383n49.

8 Legend

1. P. A. W. Collins, 'Boswell's Contact with Johnson', *Notes and Queries* 3, no. 4 (April 1956): 163–6; Donald Greene, "'Tis a Pretty Book, Mr Boswell, But –', in John A. Vance, ed., *Boswell's* Life of Johnson: *New Questions, New Answers* (Athens: The University of Georgia Press, 1985), pp. 110–46 (p. 134).
2. Hawkins, *The Life of Samuel Johnson, LL.D.*, ed. OM Brack, Jr (Athens: University of Georgia Press, 2009), p. 255.
3. Edward A. Bloom, '"As Fly Stings to a Stately Horse": Johnson under Satiric Attack', *Modern Language Studies* 9, no. 3 (1979): 137–49 (p. 137).
4. John Wiltshire, *The Making of Dr. Johnson* (Hastings: Helm Information, 2009), p. 15.
5. Charles Churchill, 'The Ghost', in *The Poetical Works of Charles Churchill*, ed. Douglas Grant (Oxford University Press, 1963), III.828–9.

6. *Monthly Review*, February 1783, vol. 68, in *Contemporary Criticisms of Johnson, His Works and His Biographers*, ed. John Ker Spittal (London: John Murray, 1923), p. 371
7. Charles Moore, 'James Boswell Revolutionised the Way We See Great Men', *Daily Telegraph*, 26 April 2013.
8. *Boswell for the Defence*, ed. William K. Wimsatt and Frederick A. Pottle (New York: McGraw-Hill, 1959), p. 83.
9. Pat Rogers, *Johnson* (Oxford University Press, 1993), p. 3.
10. Bertrand H. Bronson, 'The Double Tradition of Dr. Johnson', in *Johnson Agonistes* (Berkeley: University of California Press, 1965), pp. 156–76.
11. Isobel Grundy, 'Early Women Reading Johnson', in *Samuel Johnson After 300 Years*, ed. Greg Clingham and Philip Smallwood (Cambridge University Press, 2009), pp. 207–24 (p. 207).
12. James G. Basker, 'Multicultural Perspectives: Johnson, Race, and Gender', in *Johnson Re-Visioned: Looking Before and After*, ed. Philip Smallwood (London: Associated University Presses, 2001), pp. 64–79 (p. 68).
13. John Stone, 'Translations', in *Samuel Johnson in Context*, ed. Jack Lynch (Cambridge University Press, 2012), pp. 38–44 (p. 42).
14. See Isobel Grundy, 'Samuel Johnson as Patron of Women', *The Age of Johnson* 1 (1997), 59–77.
15. Deirdre Le Faye, *Jane Austen's Letters* (Oxford University Press, 2011), p. 126.
16. Douglas Lane Patey argues for the latter against the former in 'Johnson's Refutation of Berkeley: Kicking the Stone Again', *Journal of the History of Ideas* 47, no. 1 (1986), 139–45. As James Caudle has pointed out ('The Church's Kicked Foundation: A Concealed Johnsonian Detail', *Johnsonian News Letter* 58, no. 2 (2007), 42–48), the 'stone' was the foundation of a church and immoveable.
17. Iris Murdoch, *Metaphysics as a Guide to Morals* (London: Chatto and Windus, 1992), p. 197.
18. Marshall Waingrow, 'Boswell's Johnson', in *Twentieth-Century Interpretations of Boswell's* Life of Johnson, ed. James L. Clifford (Englewood Cliffs: Prentice-Hall, 1970), pp. 45–50: 50.
19. *The Selected Writings of William Hazlitt*, ed. Duncan Wu (London: Routledge, 1998), V.94.
20. Robert Gittings, *John Keats* (London: Little, Brown, 1968), p. 134.
21. Norman Fruman, *Coleridge: The Damaged Archangel* (London: George Allen and Unwin, 1972), p. 470n146; *Collected Letters of Samuel Taylor Coleridge*, ed. Earl Leslie Griggs (Oxford: Clarendon Press, 1966–71), II.1054.
22. *Selected Writings*, ed. Wu, I.91.
23. *Johnson: The Critical Heritage*, ed. John T. Boulton (London: Routledge and Kegan Paul, 1971), p. 8.
24. Tim Blanning, *The Romantic Revolution* (London: Weidenfeld and Nicolson, 2010), pp. 36–45; Charles Taylor, *Sources of the Self* (Cambridge, MA: Harvard University Press, 1989), pp. 368–90.

25. *The Letters of Mary Wollstonecraft Shelley*, ed. Betty T. Bennett (Baltimore: Johns Hopkins University Press, 1983), II.223.
26. Wiltshire, p. 154.
27. Ibid., pp. 155, 178n20.
28. See, e.g., Adam Rounce, 'Editions', in *Context*, ed. Lynch, pp. 31–7 (p. 34): 'Macaulay's compellingly readable demolition of the edition set in train a disastrous misreading of Johnson.'
29. G. B. Hill, *Dr. Johnson, His Friends and His Critics* (London: Smith, Elder & Co., 1878), p. 107.
30. Ibid., p. 98.
31. Thomas Babington Macaulay, *Critical and Historical Essays* (London: J. M. Dent, 1907), II.550–1.
32. *Correspondence of Horace Walpole*, ed. Wilmarth Lewis (New Haven: Yale University Press, 1937–83), XXXIX.438.
33. *Contemporary Criticisms*, ed. Spittal, p. 380.
34. *The Times*, 10 October 1884.
35. Leslie Stephen, *History of English Thought in the Eighteenth Century* (London: Smith, Elder, and Co., 1881), II.375.
36. *Fortnightly Review*, 42 (December 1884), 784; quoted in Wiltshire, p. 170.
37. 'Ink and Incapability', in Richard Curtis, *Blackadder: The Whole Damn Dynasty* (London: Michael Joseph, 1998), pp. 353–69.
38. Katherine Turner, 'The "Link of Transition": Samuel Johnson and the Victorians', in *The Victorians and the Eighteenth Century*, ed. Francis O'Gorman and Katherine Turner (London: Routledge, 2004), pp. 119–43 (p. 121).
39. Katherine Turner, 'Critical Reception to 1900', in *Context*, ed. Lynch, pp. 45–53 (p. 51).
40. Kevin Hart, *Samuel Johnson and the Culture of Property* (Cambridge University Press, 1999), pp. 60–1.
41. *Selections from Carlyle*, ed. Henry W. Boynton (Boston: Allyn and Bacon, 1896), pp. 232–4.
42. Walter Jackson Bate, *Samuel Johnson* (London: Chatto and Windus, 1978), p. 600.
43. John Ruskin, *Praeterita* (Oxford University Press, 2012), pp. 148–9.
44. Wiltshire, p. 163.
45. Walter Raleigh, *Six Essays on Johnson* (Oxford: Clarendon Press, 1910), p. 44.
46. Ibid., pp. 11, 14.
47. Ibid., p. 175.
48. Greg Clingham, 'Critical reception since 1900', in *Context*, ed. Lynch, pp. 54–61 (p. 55).
49. T. S. Eliot, 'Johnson as Critic and Poet', *On Poetry and Poets* (London: Faber & Faber, 1957), p. 169.
50. Ibid., p. 163.

51. F. R. Leavis, 'Johnson and Augustanism', in *The Common Pursuit* (London: Chatto and Windus, 1952), pp. 97–115 (p. 97).
52. F. R. Leavis, 'Johnson as Critic', in *Anna Karenina and Other Essays* (London: Chatto and Windus, 1967), pp. 197–218 (p. 197).
53. Ibid., 209.
54. Leavis, 'Johnson and Augustanism', p. 102.
55. Virginia Woolf, 'Saint Samuel of Fleet Street', in *Collected Essays* (London: Hogarth Press, 1966–7), IV.310.
56. Ibid., p. 311.
57. Jeffrey Meyers, *Samuel Johnson: The Struggle* (New York: Basic Books, 1998), pp. 457–64.
58. G. K. Chesterton, *The Common Man* (New York: Sheed and Ward, 1950), p. 121.
59. Letter to Mary Manning, 11 July 1937, cited in James Knowlson, *Damned to Fame: The Life of Samuel Beckett* (London: Bloomsbury, 1996), p. 270.
60. Kathleen M. Grange, 'Samuel Johnson's Account of Certain Psychoanalytic Concepts', in *Samuel Johnson: A Collection of Critical Essays*, ed. Donald Greene (New Jersey: Prentice-Hall, 1965), pp. 149–57.
61. Walter Jackson Bate, *Samuel Johnson* (London: Chatto and Windus, 1978), p. 27.
62. Boris Johnson, 'Dr Johnson Was a Slobbering, Sexist Xenophobe Who Understood Human Nature', *Daily Telegraph*, 14 September 2009.
63. David Hume, *Essays and Treatises on Several Subjects* (London: A. Millar, 1783), I.472.
64. A comparison drawn out by Clement Hawes, 'Johnson and Imperialism', in *The Cambridge Companion to Samuel Johnson*, ed. Greg Clingham (Cambridge University Press, 1997), pp. 114–126 (pp. 115–16).
65. Rogers, pp. 109–10.

Further Reading

Johnsonian Bibliography

Adam, R. B. *The R. B. Adam Library Relating to Dr. Samuel Johnson and His Era*. 3 vols. London: Oxford University Press, 1929.
Fleeman, J. D. *A Preliminary Handlist of Documents & Manuscripts of Samuel Johnson*. Oxford: Oxford Bibliographical Society, 1967.
   A Preliminary Handlist of Copies of Books Associated with Dr. Samuel Johnson. Oxford: Oxford Bibliographical Society, 1984.
   A Bibliography of the Works of Samuel Johnson: Treating His Published Works from the Beginnings to 1984. Prepared for publication by James McLaverty. 2 vols. Oxford University Press, 2000.
Hazen, Allen T. *Samuel Johnson's Prefaces and Dedications*. New Haven, CT: Yale University Press, 1937.

Modern Editions of Johnson's Works

A Journey to the Western Islands of Scotland, ed. J. D. Fleeman. Oxford University Press, 1985.
The Latin and Greek Poems of Samuel Johnson, ed. Barry Baldwin. London: Duckworth, 1995.
The Letters of Samuel Johnson, ed. Bruce Redford. 5 vols. Princeton University Press, 1992–4.
The Poems of Samuel Johnson, ed. David Nichol Smith and Edward L. McAdam. 2nd ed. Oxford University Press, 1974.
Samuel Johnson: Selected Works, ed. Robert DeMaria, Jr, Steven Fix, and Howard Weinbrot. New Haven, CT: Yale University Press, 2021.
Samuel Johnson: The Complete Poems of Samuel Johnson, ed. Robert D. Brown and Robert DeMaria, Jr. London: Routledge, 2024.
Samuel Johnson: The Lives of the Most Eminent English Poets: With Critical Observations on Their Works, ed. Roger Lonsdale. 4 vols. Oxford: Clarendon Press, 2006.
Samuel Johnson: The Major Works, ed. Donald Greene. Oxford University Press, 1984.

The Yale Edition of the Works of Samuel Johnson, ed. Robert DeMaria, Jr, Allen T. Hazen, John H. Middendorf, et al. 23 vols. New Haven, CT: Yale University Press, 1958–2019.

Biographical Studies

Bate, W. Jackson. *Samuel Johnson*. New York: Harcourt, 1977.
Boswell, James. *The Life of Samuel Johnson, LL.D.* (orig. pub. 1791), ed. G. B. Hill, revised and enlarged L. F. Powell. 6 vols. Oxford: Clarendon Press, 1934–64.
Brack, O. M., Jr, and Robert E. Kelley, eds. *The Early Biographies of Samuel Johnson*. Iowa City: University of Iowa Press, 1974.
DeMaria, Robert, Jr. *The Life of Samuel Johnson: A Critical Biography*. Oxford: Clarendon Press, 1993.
Hawkins, Sir John, *The Life of Samuel Johnson, LL.D.*, ed. O. M. Brack, Jr. Athens: University of Georgia Press, 2009.
Hill, George Birkbeck, ed. *Johnsonian Miscellanies*. 2 vols. Oxford University Press, 1897.
Kaminski, Thomas. *The Early Career of Samuel Johnson*. Oxford University Press, 1987.
Lipking, Lawrence. *Samuel Johnson: The Life of an Author*. Cambridge, MA: Harvard University Press, 1988.
Nokes, David. *Samuel Johnson, A Life*. New York: Henry Holt, 2010.
Piozzi, Hester Lynch. *Anecdotes of the Late Samuel Johnson, LL.D.* London, 1786.
Reade, Aleyn Lyell. *Johnsonian Gleanings*, 11 vols. (1909–52); repr. New York: Octagon Books, 1968.
Wain, John. *Samuel Johnson*. London: Macmillan, 1974.
Wiltshire, John. *The Making of Dr. Johnson*. Hastings: Helm Information, 2009.
Yung, Kai Kin. *Samuel Johnson 1709–84*. London: Herbert Press, 1984.

Johnson's Books, His Friends, and His Times

Bundock, Michael. *The Fortunes of Francis Barber*. New Haven, CT: Yale University Press, 2015.
Clifford, James L. *Hester Lynch Piozzi (Mrs. Thrale)*. Oxford University Press, 1941.
DeMaria, Robert, Jr. *Samuel Johnson and the Life of Reading*. Baltimore: Johns Hopkins University Press, 1997.
Deutsch, Helen. *Loving Dr. Johnson*. University of Chicago Press, 2005.
Greene, Donald. *Samuel Johnson's Library: An Annotated Guide*. University of Victoria Press, 1975.
Hudson, Nicholas. *Samuel Johnson and Eighteenth-Century Thought*. Oxford: Clarendon Press, 1988.
Lynch, Jack, ed. *Samuel Johnson in Context*. Cambridge University Press, 2012.

General Critical Studies of Johnson, including Collections of Essays

Bronson, Bertrand H. *Johnson Agonistes & Other Essays*. Berkeley: University of California Press, 1946.

Clingham, Greg, ed. *The Cambridge Companion to Samuel Johnson*, Cambridge University Press, 1997.

The New Cambridge Companion to Samuel Johnson. Cambridge University Press, 2023.

Grundy, Isobel. *Samuel Johnson and the Scale of Greatness*. Leicester University Press, 1986.

Hilles, Frederick W., ed. *New Light on Dr. Johnson: Essays on the Occasion of his 250th Birthday*. New Haven, CT: Yale University Press, 1959.

Johnsonian News Letter, ed. James Clifford, John Middendorf, and Robert DeMaria, Jr. 1940–.

Johnston, Freya. *Samuel Johnson and the Art of Sinking, 1709–1791*. Oxford University Press, 2005.

Johnston, Freya and Lynda Mugglestone, eds. *Samuel Johnson: The Arc of the Pendulum*. Oxford University Press, 2012.

Korshin, Paul, ed. *Johnson after Two Hundred Years*. Oxford University Press, 1986.

Korshin, Paul, Jack Lynch, and John Scanlan, eds. *The Age of Johnson*. New Brunswick: Rutgers University Press, 1998–.

Lipking, Lawrence. 'Learning to Read Johnson: *The Vision of Theodore* and the *Vanity of Human Wishes*'. *ELH* 43, no. 4 (1976): 517–37.

Lynch, Jack, ed. *The Oxford Handbook of Samuel Johnson*. Oxford University Press, 2022.

Rogers, Pat. *Samuel Johnson*. Oxford University Press, 1993.

The Samuel Johnson Encyclopedia. Westport, CT: Greenwood Press, 1996.

Weinbrot, Howard, ed. *Samuel Johnson: New Contexts for a New Century*. San Marino: Huntington Library, 2011.

Specialized Studies

Brownell, Morris R. *Samuel Johnson's Attitude to the Arts*. Oxford: Clarendon Press, 1989.

DeMaria, Robert, Jr. *Johnson's Dictionary and the Language of Learning*. Oxford: Clarendon Press, 1986.

Eliot, T. S. Introductory essay to *London: A Poem and The Vanity of Human Wishes*. London: Hazelwood Press, 1930.

Fleeman, J. D. 'Johnson's Poetry'. *Proceedings of the British Academy* 69 (1983): 355–69.

Hudson, Nicholas. *A Political Biography of Samuel Johnson*. London: Routledge, 2013.

Mugglestone, Lynda. *Samuel Johnson and the Journey into Words*. Oxford University Press, 2015.
Reddick, Allen. *The Making of Johnson's Dictionary, 1746–1773*. 2nd ed. Cambridge University Press, 1996.
Rees, Christine. *Johnson's Milton*. Cambridge University Press, 2010.
Samuel Johnson Dictionary Sources, ed. Brian K. Grimes. www.sjdictionarysources.org/.
Venturo, David. *Johnson the Poet*. London: Associated University Press, 1999.
Wimsatt, William K. *Philosophic Words*. New Haven, CT: Yale University Press, 1948.

Index

Addison, Joseph, 1, 46, 61
Anne, Queen of England, 1
Arnold, Matthew, 143
Austen, Jane, 139

Barber, Francis, 13, 17, 21
Baretti, Giuseppe, 17, 19
Barry, James, 145
Bate, Walter Jackson, 144
Beckett, Samuel, 60, 147
Bentley, Richard, 62, 71, 72
Birch, Thomas, 10, 11, 12, 74
Birmingham Journal, 8
Blackadder, 143
Blair, Hugh, 140
Bloom, Harold, 79
Boileau-Despréaux, Nicolas, 48
Boothby, Hill, 3, 15
Boswell & Johnson's Scottish Road Trip, 148
Boswell, James, 18, 19, 21, 22, 44, 59, 61, 73, 105, 133, 136–8
  Journal of a Tour to the Hebrides, 110
  Life of Johnson, 78, 82, 133, 134, 139–41, 145
Burke, Edmund, 99
Burney, Charles, 41

Callender, John, 135
capital punishment, 101
Carlyle, Thomas, 144
Carter, Elizabeth, 10, 47
Cave, Edward, 8, 9, 23–7, 62; *see also Gentleman's Magazine*
Chambers, Robert, 106

Chesterfield, Lord, 13, 14, 53, 145
Chesterton, G. K., 147
Churchill, Charles, 135
Club, The, 133
Coleridge, Samuel Taylor, 79
common reader, the, 89–91
Croft, Herbert, 127
Croker, John Wilson, 142

Davies, Thomas, 137
debtors' prisons, 99
Dodsley, Robert, 11, 12, 14, 16, 47, 48
Dryden, John, 2

Edial, 9, 23
Eliot, T. S., 146

Fielding, Henry, 101
Ford, Cornelius, 6

Garrick, David, 9, 10, 14, 44, 63, 137
general nature, 86–7, 88
Gentleman's Magazine, 8, 10, 11, 23–7, 47, 62
Gloucester Journal, 27
Goldsmith, Oliver, 149
Gordon Riots, 103
Gosse, Edmund, 143
Gough Square, 12, 17, 19
Gray, Thomas, 55, 62
Grub Street, 26, 70

Hammond, Henry, 3
Hanway, Jonas, 40
Harleian Library, 11

Hawkesworth, John, 24
Hawkins, John, 133
    Life of Johnson, 133
Hazlitt, William, 141
Hector, Edmund, 5, 6
Herrick, George, 49
Hill, G. B., 142, 145
Horace, 1
Hume, David, 148

Ivy Lane Club, 133

Jacobites, 2, 38, 102, 104
Jenyns, Soame, 40, 99–100
Johnson, Elizabeth Porter (née Jervis), 8, 10, 13, 15
Johnson, Nathaniel, 5, 9
Johnson, Samuel
    charity, 3
    compassion, 100
    disabilities, 5
    earnings, 24, 58
    marriage, 8, 13
    melancholy, 5
    parents, 6, 8
    pension, 17, 71, 106
    poetry defined by, 44
    politics, 2, 10
    psychological conditions, 5
    reading
        Pilgrim's Progress, 4
        revealed in his *Dictionary*, 2
        voluminous, 37
    religion, 2, 36, 54, 102
        evangelicalism, 3
        fear of damnation, 4
        melancholy, 3
        orthodoxy, 3
        scruples, 4, 15
    women regarded by, 139
    works
        'Ad Urbanum', 24
        Adventurer, 37
        book reviews, 39–40

Compleat Vindication of the Licensers of the Stage, 10, 104, 105
Crousaz's *Commentary*, 24
'Debates in the Senate of Magna Lilliputia', 28
definitions in the *Dictionary*, 69–70
Dictionary of the English Language, 12, 13, 14, 16, 17, 18, 54, 55, 60, 62, 63–71, 81
epitaph on a duck, 43
etymologies in the *Dictionary*, 67
False Alarm, The, 20, 102, 107–8
footnotes, 76
'Fountains, The', 56
Harleian Catalogue, 63
History of the Council of Trent, 24, 62
Idler, 16, 17, 37, 38–9, 47, 71
'In theatro', 65
Irene, 8, 9, 10, 14
Journey to the Western Islands, 19, 20, 110–12
'Know thyself', 54, 77
'Life of Ascham', 124, 130
'Life of Akenside', 88
'Life of Baratier', 118
Life of Boerhaave, 116
'Life of Browne', 116
'Life of Cave', 120
'Life of Cheynell', 117
'Life of Confucius', 117
'Life of Cowley', 84, 88
'Life of Drake', 118
'Life of Dryden', 84, 123, 126, 127
'Life of Gray', 90
'Life of Hermann Boerhaave', 80, 83
'Life of Milton', 117, 128–30
'Life of Pope', 83, 85, 126, 127
'Life of Rochester', 127
'Life of Swift', 84, 126
'Life of Sydenham', 118

Johnson, Samuel (cont.)
   'Life of Waller', 128
   Life of Savage, 120–2, 127
   lines contributed to Goldsmith's *The Traveller*, 112
   Lives of the Poets, 1, 3, 20, 81, 127–30
   London, 7, 10, 14, 17, 47–50, 104
   Marmor Norfolciense, 10
   Miscellaneous Observations on the Tragedy of Macbeth, 63
   Observations on the Present State of Affairs, 106
   'On the Death of Robert Levet', 21, 54–5
   'Of the Duty of a Journalist', 26
   'Pamphilus on Condolence', 25
   parody of Bishop Percy's ballad 'The Hermit of Warkworth', 44
   parody of Thomas Warton's verse, 44
   Patriot, The, 20, 108, 109–10
   Plan of a Dictionary, 13
   Plays of William Shakespeare, 11, 16, 17, 18, 62, 76
   prayers, 16, 22, 45–6, 55
   Preface to Shakespeare, 79, 83, 84, 85
   Rambler, 15, 16, 36, 51, 56, 58, 59, 83, 91
   Rasselas, 8, 60, 87, 130, 143
   'Reflections on the present state of literature', 26
   review of the Duchess of Marlborough's Memoirs, 29, 80
   sermons, 15
   'Somnium', 7
   Taxation No Tyranny, 20, 108–9
   Thoughts on Falkland's Islands, 20, 101, 108, 110
   translation of Addison's 'Pygmies and Cranes', 46
   translation of Pope's *Messiah*, 7, 46
   translation of *The History of the Council of Trent*, 9
   translations of the *Greek Anthology*, 45
   Vanity of Human Wishes, The, 7, 10, 14, 54, 56, 73
   'Vision of Theodore, the Hermit of Teneriffe, The', 12, 57
   Voyage to Abyssinia, 8, 58
   'Young Author, The', 7, 46–7
Johnson's Court, 17
Junius, Franciscus, 67
Juvenal, 10, 48, 51, 53

Keats, John, 141

Langton, Bennet, 133
Leavis, F. R., 146
Levet, Robert, 12, 21, 55
Lichfield Grammar School, 1, 6, 61
Literary Magazine, 16, 27, 39, 71

Macaulay, Lord, 67, 142, 143
metaphysical poets, 88
Milton, John
   Paradise Lost, 80, 94
monarchy, 102
Monthly Review, 143
More, Hannah, 139
Mudge, Zachariah, 117
Murdoch, Iris, 140

Nabokov, Vladimir, 147
Nichols, John, 123
novels, 115

Oldham, John, 48
Oxford University, 6, 7

Parr, Samuel, 61, 136
patriotism, 105
patronage, 11, 14; *see also* Chesterfield
Piozzi, Hester Thrale, 9, 18–19, 73, 134, 136

Topics

American Literary Realism Phillip Barrish

American Poetry Since 1945 Andrew Epstein

The American Short Story Martin Scofield

Anglo-Saxon Literature Hugh Magennis

British Fiction, 1900–1950 Robert L. Caserio

British Poetry, 1945–2010 Eric Falci

Comedy Eric Weitz

Contemporary American Fiction Stacey Olster

Creative Writing David Morley

Early English Theatre Janette Dillon

Early Modern Drama, 1576–1642 Julie Sanders

The Eighteenth-Century Novel April London

Eighteenth-Century Poetry John Sitter

English Theatre, 1660–1900 Peter Thomson

Francophone Literature Patrick Corcoran

French Literature Brian Nelson

German Poetry Judith Ryan

Literary Posthumanism Joseph Tabbi

Literature and the Environment Timothy Clark

Modern British Theatre Simon Shepherd

Modern Irish Poetry Justin Quinn

Modernism Pericles Lewis

Modernist Poetry Peter Howarth

Narrative (second edition) H. Porter Abbott

Narrative (third edition) H. Porter Abbott

The Nineteenth-Century American Novel Gregg Crane

The Novel Marina MacKay

Old Norse Sagas Margaret Clunies Ross

Performance Theory Simon Shepherd

Postcolonial Literatures C. L. Innes

Postmodern Fiction Bran Nicol

Romantic Poetry Michael Ferber

Russian Literature Caryl Emerson

Satire Jonathan Greenberg

Scenography Joslin McKinney and Philip Butterworth

The Short Story in English Adrian Hunter

Theatre and Literature of the Absurd Michael Y. Bennett

Theatre Directing Christopher Innes and Maria Shevtsova

Theatre Historiography Thomas Postlewait

Theatre Studies Christopher B. Balme

Tragedy Jennifer Wallace

Victorian Poetry Linda K. Hughes

www.ingramcontent.com/pod-product-compliance
Ingram Content Group UK Ltd.
Pitfield, Milton Keynes, MK11 3LW, UK
UKHW030743110225
454939UK00012B/148